Steve Toogood.

20 Newport

Lincoln

LN1 3DF.

APRIL

CW00601206

FRENCH FAÏENCE
Fantaisie et Populaire
of the 19th and 20th Centuries

by Millicent S. Mali

United Printing

Dedication

To Pierre for his constant encouragement and support.

Cover Photograph: **Quimper** Vase 11 ¼" tall. Blue *décor riche* on yellow background. Alfred Beau design: *"Retour du Pardon"*. Porquier factory. Late 19th cent. (Private Collection)

Malicorne Cup and saucer. Peasant figures and florals copied from Quimper. Pouplard factory. Late 19th cent. (Private Collection)

Desvres Clock case 9¼" tall. Fourmaintraux-Courquin factory. Early 20th cent. (Private Collection)

CA Holy water font *bénitier de chevet* 5" tall (Private Collection)

Photography by Angell Photography

Graphics by Island Graphics and Creative Typesetting

ISBN 0-9603824-2-9

CONTENTS

Acknowledgements

Many friends, dealers and fellow collectors have encouraged me to pursue this research, but it would not have been possible without the gracious assistance of the faienciers who gave me access to their factories, their museums and their special knowledge. My deep appreciation to Pierre Henriot, Bernard Verlingue, Mme Jules Verlingue, Alain Henriot, Philippe Lalys at the Quimper factory; also to Michel Roullot whose expert knowledge of antique Quimper assisted me greatly. At the St. Clément factory: M. Doucet. At Malicorne: M. and Mme. Despres and M. Victor Deschang. At Desvres: M. Guislain Delassus, M. Jacques Guillerme. Also my deepest thanks to Philippe Knoblock, who gave so generously of his time and assistance often at moments inconvenient to him.

Among the museum curators who were most helpful my thanks go to Mme Antoinette Hallé at Sèvres, Mme Oger at Tours, Mme Vaudour at Rouen, and especially Mme Martine de Mallerais at Blois.

To M. Robert Bouchet of the Chambre Syndicale Française de la Céramique who in our behalf contacted his friend M. Fourest, the past curator of Sèvres, my deep appreciation for his interest.

To Mme. Ginette Noël and M. André Laflamme of the Division des Archives, Ville de Québec; also to M. André Cochrane of the Bibliothèque de l'Assemblée Nationale, our gratitude for their help.

Finally to Ruth and Chris whose able assistance in getting this manuscript together has been invaluable, I want to thank them again for their creative ideas, their enthusiasm and unfailing good humor throughout all our trials.

Millicent S. Mali

East Greenwich
July 1986

Foreword

This book is written primarily for the American collector whose knowledge of French faience lags behind his love and appreciation for the colorful, warm and appealing pottery. Since 17th and 18th century French faience is found mostly in museums today, the chances of the casual collector's finding these pieces in the street markets or at country auctions are remote indeed. Rather, the items which appear today at affordable prices are articles generally from the late 19th and early 20th centuries, made in a number of small French *fabriques.* I have translated this word in the text as factory, meaning both large and small concerns. Also I have used the French word *faïencerie* meaning a factory which produces *faïence.* In both cases, I have opted throughout the text to use the American spelling except when these words occur in a specific French title.

The initial chapters present a very brief introduction to basic phrases, definitions and styles which characterize 17th and 18th century French faience. I describe the history of the great potting centers: Rouen, Nevers, Moustiers, Strasbourg, and Marseilles, only to point out briefly how they evolved and which particular decorative themes or techniques they contributed to the repertoire and the development of faience in general. For more information on 17th and 18th century French faience, consult the Bibliography.

The second and main portion of the book reports on faience of the late 19th and early 20th centuries — not so much the development of art pottery, those exciting contributions of various individuals who experimented with *grès* ware in *art nouveau* and *art déco* forms — but those examples which have come to be called *fantaisie* and souvenir items.

At the turn of the present century, the artistic movement appeared to be going in two opposite directions. One school of thought answered the call for a return to the simple and basic. Their aim was to see the harmonious application of clay, paint, wood, fibre, paper, etc. made into useful as well as decorative forms. This was the Modern Movement. Art potters, such as Bigot, Delaherche, Carriès, Massier, etc. fall into this category. The other direction was sentimental, historic and *passéist.* This group called for the revival of the old; a harkening back to the past and the great glories of the 18th century. This revival occured in architecture, furniture, etc., as well as in faience making.

The advances of technology which had initially destroyed, by rendering unprofitable, the great decorative art of the 18th century, now produced such changes in the economy, social mobility and popular taste that there arose a new desire and a new clientele for reproductions. The old faience was revived, similar yet different, for now it came in the shape of mementoes and souvenirs, often bearing the name of a resort town. The faience appeared as *fantaisie* pieces, whimsical figurines, animal shapes, miniatures and simplified copies of prestigious originals.

Though the experts have considered these popular, actually commercial faiences as second-rate and unimportant because they come under the heading of bric-a-brac, rather than "art", I have chosen to write about them for several reasons. These commercial products are more plentiful in the markets than the older, more distinguished faiences. They have developed a certain following and collectors are accumulating pieces which they are now anxious to identify. More importantly, I have researched these products because I feel they have been slighted. No information has been compiled on the various factories. Outside of random magazine articles and on-site investigation, reference material and expert help has been almost totally lacking. Many of these faiences are getting to be a hundred years old, some even older, and are no longer being produced. While age is not in itself an indicator of value, the production of these items, their designs and models, tell us much about the social and cultural influences which spawned them. We should know about them.

I hope this research will aid the collectors to identify and learn about some of their choice items. I trust that the marks and signatures I have included here will clarify the age and origins of these pieces.

Boulogne-sur-Mer
Desvres
Rouen
Caen
Creil
Sarreguemines
St. Clément
Lunéville
Strasbourg
Paris
Seine
Quimper
Rennes
Sarthe
Malicorne
Loire
Blois
Gien
Tours
Nevers
Limoges
Angoulême
Lyon
Garonne
Moustiers
Marseille

Introduction

What is Faience?

Faience, majolica and delftware are all terms which refer to an earthenware product covered with a tin-enameled (stanniferous) glaze which became popular in Europe in the 16th and early 17th centuries. These terms are associated with the towns or areas which manufactured them. Thus, majolica is a corruption of Majorca, which was the center for the production of Hispano-Moresque ware. It is the earliest form of the three types, introduced into Italy in the 15th century.

Delftware refers to the white enameled, blue monochrome, early 17th century reproductions of those Chinese porcelains which came to the West in the ships of the Dutch East India Company. Dutch potters in and around Delft imitated the designs and forms of the original Chinese and Japanese plates and vases, lending the name delftware to these earthenware products.

Likewise, the term faience refers to the white enameled pottery produced in the 16th century in the small Italian town of Faenza (not to be confused with Florence (Firenza).

This Italian pottery, or faience as it came to be called in France, was composed of a mixture of local clays, which were beaten, picked over to remove impurities, mixed with water and put through a sieve. The cleansed clay was left to dry. In France the mixture was known as *pâte.* Made up of *argile* or a fire clay and *marne,* which translates as marls, this clay contained a high percentage of carbonate of lime which when fired became pinky red or buff in color depending on other elements in the clay. The biscuit or product of the first firing was very strong, yet light in weight.

Tin-Enamel Glaze

During the 15th century, knowledge of tin-enamel glazing traveled westward from Persia, through the Middle East and the Islamic World to Spain and Italy. This glaze, originally a secret of Babylonian potters, required the piece to be fired at a higher temperature than the ordinary pottery or *terre cuite.* Unfortunately, this high degree of heat (1000°) often caused the clay body to crumble, ruining the piece. However, not until a clever, unknown potter of Faenza had solved the problem by adding feldspar to the basic clays could the new ceramic product, faience, be efficiently and economically produced.

The new *pâte,* now containing feldspar, covered with the stanniferous glaze proved a sturdy product whose decoration did not discolor as the earlier lead glazes had. New possibilities for color and design opened up.

The tin glaze was prepared by combining melted, clean siliceous sand and the potash salt left from wine sediment with lead and tin ashes in a 30/12 part formula. The white enamel which was thus formed could be applied on the raw clay, painted then fired. Or the piece could be enameled, baked at a high temperature, painted and then baked again at a lower temperature. In the firing, the tin oxide created a uniform white surface which was more opaque and less glossy than that of the lead glaze. This matte surface provided a superior foundation for color.

The pigments used with the early tin-enamel glaze were compounded from metallic oxides or earths. Yellow was made of antimony of lead; this mixed with oxide of iron would make orange. Green was made from oxide of copper; blue from oxide of cobalt; purple from manganese. Red was a particularly difficult color to achieve. Tricky and unreliable, it would frequently turn drab brown in the firing, flake or fade out. Red does not appear in early Nevers ware; it was used sparingly and with special application in the Rouen faiences.

Grand Feu

The Italian and French faiences of the 16th, 17th and early 18th centuries were produced by the *grand feu* method. According to this technique, the clay piece was fired once (biscuit) and then dipped or covered with a liquid glaze. When the raw glaze had dried to a powdery surface, the artist painted his design. This procedure was very exacting — no change or correction could be made without smudging the surface. The pieces were then fired a second time at 920° - 960°. This bonded the glaze to the piece and activated the mineral salts so that the colors came alive. But, as has already been noted, the red was usually the most difficult to achieve. Other colors: purples, pinks, certain greens and gold were not possible until the discovery of the *petit feu* method.

Petit Feu

Around the middle of the 18th century, a Strasbourg faiencier developed the technique of the *petit feu* which he learned from German immigrants. This method entailed two more procedures: 1) the use of a *fondant* (flux) and, 2) a third firing. In the *petit feu* method, the biscuit would be glazed and fired before the decoration was applied. Then paints, mixed with a colorless flux were used on top of the "cooked" glaze and the piece was fired a third time at a reduced temperature (750° - 800°) in a specially constructed, muffle kiln. The faience of Strasbourg and the eastern centers were made by this process.

Faïence Fine

Best known for its affiliation with English factories and English operated French factories, *faïence fine* was composed of a very white clay and a very fine sand. The biscuit was covered with a simple, translucent glaze. The decoration was painted or stenciled on top of the glaze, then fired gently. In France, *faïence fine* appeared first in Sceaux in the 18th century; but the Creil-Montereau factories, particularly during the 19th century are the most well known for this product.

Grès

Grès describes a pottery made of a very hard clay which fires to a dense, sturdy product. Because the clay mixture is different from the clay used in faience making, *grès* is not considered a true faience. Originally, *grès* ware was used like stoneware for utilitarian purposes. It was cheap to produce as only one firing was necessary. Later, *grès* ware became an art form when the addition of a thin glaze, *vernis,* (either clear or tinted) and a second firing changed the color and texture of the finished piece. Sometimes a salt glaze was used on a *grès* base. This was achieved by throwing sea salt into the kiln during the firing cycle.

The History of Faience

The history of the development of pottery follows two, often diverse trends. One is the use of ceramics as pure decoration; the second is the production of pottery as functional household items. These two ideologies combine and separate throughout ceramic history. Periods of "art for art's sake" are interspersed with utilitarian influences and later, in the 19th century, efforts will emerge to combine artistic expression into industrial and commercial products.

As the forerunner of Italian, then French faience, tin-glazed pottery from the Middle East was intended primarily as decoration. In keeping with Islamic law forbidding the reproduction of the human figure, the Hispano-Moresque potters used the following motifs: natural flowers, imaginative flowers, scroll-work, arabesques and geometrical designs, animals and birds. The shapes they used included jugs, mugs, plates and occasionally lamps for mosques and covered bowls. These themes will be seen repeatedly throughout the development of French faience.

One of the great effects of the Renaissance movement in late 15th century Italy, was the flowering of the spirit of individuality, which in the art fields led to new creativity, new combinations of form, fabric and function. Italian craftsmen of this period looked across the traditional trade lines and ignored constricting influences of the old guilds. Sculptors, like Della Robbia included majolica ornamentation with his figures. Potters turned to painters to provide finer decoration on their basic albarelli (pharmacy pots) or dramatic scenes on their large ornamental plates. The range of color and decoration progressed rapidly until the towns of Gubbio, Urbino, Faenza, Siena, Deruta became the chief centers of the *stile bello* and the *stile istoriati* pottery which influenced French faience so greatly.

Stile Bello

The *stile bello* decoration consisted of a central medallion or cartouche, surrounded by a secondary motif: garlands, symetric scrolls or designs.

Stile Istoriati

The *stile istoriati* decoration featured a scene from history, mythology, religion or Bible story inspired by the works of other painters or famous engravers and recreated on faience by hand. Given as gifts on special occasions, such as births and marriages, these articles popularized the fine arts and spread culture in the early 16th century. Unlike the *stile bello,* the decoration of the *stile istoriati* covered the entire plate to a narrow band around the edge. The background was often composed of waves, undulating strokes depicting the ocean; or, countryside scenes, hazy landscapes contrasting the prominent figures in the foreground.

As the style progressed, different artistic elements were mingled in a free association over the full surface of the piece. Cupids and satyrs from classical mythology, grotesques and winged animals, abstract geometrical forms and allegorical figures would combine in a rich tapestry of color and design.

In contrast to this very ornate style of the Urbino school, the *compendiario* technique from Faenza, consisted of minimal decoration. The scene painted with a few brush strokes on a white background stood out as refreshingly delicate and uncluttered.

These are the decorative styles which crossed into France in the mid-16th century and began to appear in the pottery of Lyons. However, the faience trade did not thrive in this city. Continuing wars which interrupted commerce, combined with the extremely high cost of faience production in Lyons caused those potters to migrate inland to Nevers where much more favorable conditions prevailed. There they found an excellent clay for firing, and a local sand which formed a remarkable bond between the biscuit and the glaze. The ease of transportation along the Loire river toward new markets in the West, added to the enlightened patronage of the duc de Nevers determined the establishment of Italian artists in this region in the early 17th century. Thus began the extraordinary art form which was the glory of France in the 18th century.

PART I

The Histories of *les Cinq Grands*

Nevers
Rouen
Moustiers/Marseilles
Strasbourg

Decline of French Faience

"The Clothes of a Glassmaker/Faiencier"

It was not unusual for an artisan to work in both trades. They had much in common. Both were considered basic creations of earth and fire; both used the same silica-rich sand and fire clay for the process. In the 16th century, glassmakers from Faenza, Venice and Florence also made faience; the artists would often pass from one craft to the other without difficulty. Under the protection of the duc de Nevers, a section of Nevers was named "petit Murano" for the Italian glassworkers who settled there.

Nevers

The geographic situation of Nevers at the confluence of the Nievre and the Loire rivers only partially explains the establishment of Nevers as a great potting center. The province of Nevers was governed by an Italian patron, Lodovico Gonzaga, a soldier of fortune who became duc de Nevers by virtue of his marriage to Henriette of Cleves. This prince, the godfather of Catherine de Medici, son of the duc of Mantua, surrounded himself with artists and savants.

In 1588, a contract signed between Augustin Conrade (native of Albissola, near Savona) and Julio Gambin (formerly Guilio Gambini) a painter originally from Faenza, but lately from Lyons, formed an association under the protection of the duc. This association which continued through several generations until 1672, produced the style of pottery known as italo-nivernais, which much resembled the *stile bello* and *stile istoriati* of Urbino and Florence. They also created a series of products—vases, pitchers, platters, etc. in a cameo blue monochrome decoration which was related to monochrome work done in Savona, the elder Conrade's homeland. "Grotesques", figures, hares, birds and serpents appear in the decoration during this period and resemble later grotesque figures which appear in the faience of Moustiers.

2. **Nevers** Covered vase, 9" tall. Persian blue decoration with white overpainting, (Courtesy C. Massin, Les Faïences de Nevers)

The Italian tradition persisted until 1630 or thereabouts. Then, Genoese and Venetian trade with the East brought Persian goods into the marketplace. New designs found on the imported fabrics inspired the painters and potters with new forms, new colors and new interpretations of flowers, birds, and decorative detail that could be used on ceramics.

The Persian Period (1630 - 1710)

Three types of faience issued from the Persian period.

1) **the Persian Blue** — a very dark blue glaze background with white or yellow overpainted in designs of flowers, birds and insects.
2) **Green Décor** — a white glaze decorated with flowers in a green color made from copper oxides.
3) **Yellow Décor** — very rare. A yellow glaze with white and blue overpaint, usually in a floral design.

The Chinese Period (1660 - 1760)

The appearance of porcelains from China and the Far East inspired an important period of imitation and interpretation which spread throughout the potting centers of France. Nevers which initiated the style had had early access to oriental shapes and forms through the Genoese and Venetian trade. Now the Dutch East India Company's imports brought Chinese decorations to other centers in France. Sometimes decorating oriental forms, other times found on Italian or local French molds, the Chinese motifs became very popular and took over the imagination of the French collector. *Chinoiserie* eclipsed the Italian style and spread rapidly to Rouen, Moustiers and Strasbourg.

3. **Nevers** Chevrette (apothecary vase for the storage of medicinal syrups). Green *décor* of the Persian period. (Courtesy C. Massin, Les Faïences de Nevers)

4. **Nevers** Flower holder, *pique-fleurs*, in rare yellow *décor*. (Courtesy C. Massin, Les Faïences de Nevers)

Faience objects which were characteristic of Nevers production included statues of the Virgin and many of the saints; other religious items, such as holy water fonts and church vessels.

At the end of the 18th century, Nevers produced a series of revolutionary plates. These were a popular faience with patriotic themes which can almost trace the development of the French Revolution. In a sense they became the first of the faience souvenirs — objects of instruction as well as *aide-mémoires.*

In 1789, plates with the following mottos appeared:

"La Réunion des Etats Généraux"
"La Déclaration des Droits de l'Homme"
"La Prise de la Bastille"
"Le Repas des Guards du Corps"

In 1790:
"La Fête de la Fédération"

In 1791:
"La Nouvelle Constitution"
"La Mort de Mirabeau"
"La Fonte des Trésors de l'Eglise"
"Le Serment constitutionel des Prêtres"

In 1792:
"La Plantation des Arbres de la Liberté"
"L'Emission des Assignats"
"L'Attaque des Tuileries"
"La Proclamation de la République"

In 1793:
"Les Luttes de la Convention"

In 1794:
"La Paix"

5. Nevers Revolutionary plate showing the union of the three orders. The people are represented by the sheaf of wheat; the nobility, by the sword and the clergy, by the crosier. (Courtesy C. Massin, Les Faïences de Nevers)

With various symbols painted into the designs, these plates celebrated the union of the people, the bravery of their armies and the end of royal oppression. Some of the symbols were:

an anchor — hope
broken chains — deliverance
a caduceus — peace
scales — justice
laurel wreath — victory
a sword — nobility
a cross — clergy
wheat sheaves — abundance, or the people
a bundle of sticks — union, accord
the Phrygian cap — liberty.

An interesting note: the Phrygian cap was a soft, red conical hat worn by workmen or farmers. Also called a red bonnet, it became a symbol of resistance and liberty; those who wore it were known as Red Bonnets. Though the symbol figures repeatedly in the Nevers Revolutionary designs, the Phrygian cap is always painted yellow. The faienciers of Nevers had not yet mastered the color red.

In 1860 M. Champfleury, the curator of the Sèvres museum, published a study of these faiences. His interest in the subject and style of the plates sparked other potting centers to reproduce and distribute them as old examples. Most of the revolutionary plates that collectors find today are 19th century, or later, copies of the 18th century Nevers products.

In 1789, a *cahier de doléances,* or notebook of grievances was drawn up by the master potters to be presented at the convention of the Estates General. This petition for the abrogation of the 1786 Treaty listed sixty-five, well-reputed manufacturers in the country. Each factory employed more than fifty workers. Nevers claimed twelve such establishments. They were:

1) Conrade-Garillaud, Hudes .... rue St. Genest
2) Custode (L'Autruche) .... rue St. Genest
3) Estienne (Ecco Homo) .... rue St. Genest
4) Moreau, Champesle, Dumont .... rue de la Tartre
5) Bethleem (joined in 1809 to factory above)
6) Halle .... rue de la Tartre
7) Bouzeau-Deville .... rue de la Tartre
8) Ollivier .... rue de la Tartre
9) Gounot .... rue de la Cathedral
10) Chazelle, bonnaire
(La Fleur de Lys) .... Place Mosse
11) (Bout du Monde) .... rue de la Porte du Groux
12) (La Royale) .... rue des Grillots (du Singe)

During the next ten years (1790 - 1800) many changes occured in the town. The duchy of Nevers was joined to the French Republic. A serious flood ruined the port of Nevers and destroyed the wood supply for the furnaces. In 1791, six factories had gone under; the other six were working at half their earlier capacity. A commission was formed to try to restore the devastated industry, but war and loss of patronage overwhelmed the commission's efforts. Gradually the faienceries closed down. Between 1816 and 1826, fifty workers left Nevers for other potting centers in France. By 1859 only four factories remained. Today *Bout du Monde,* directed by Montagnon is the only surviving faiencerie in Nevers.

The mark of the Montagnon factory is composed of a green bow which forms a rebus. There are two versions of this pictorial representation: 1) According to Chaffers, *Mon taignon* means my tie and suggests the owner's name, Montagnon. 2) The second version is *Noeud vert,* meaning green bow which suggests the name of the town, Nevers.

Some of Montagnon's marks:

Antoine Montagnon
(1875 - 1889)

Antoine Montagnon
(1889 - 1899)

Gabriel Montagnon
(1899 - 1937)

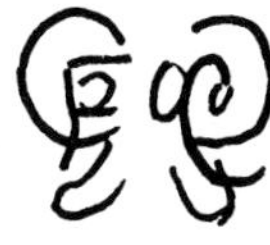

F.E. Cottard
1922

Jean Montagnon
(1937 - 1978)

6. Korea Vase, 18" tall, 17th cent., showing the dragon, Lung, emblem of the Emperor, symbol of spring and herald of storms. Lung had the head of a camel, horns like a deer, the belly of a frog, feet like a tiger and five claws, indicating a person of highest rank. (Courtesy Musée de la Céramique, Rouen, Photo: Ellebé)

7. Rouen Platter, French interpretation of the Oriental dragon, Lung. 18th cent. (Musée de la Céramique, Rouen)

8. Desvres Plate, 9 ¾ diameter, probably Fourmaintraux-Courquin factory. This example is copied from an earlier Quimper version; note: Breton shield at top. Early 20th cent.

9. Quimper Platter *"á la guivre" décor* patterned on earlier Rouen design (See Plate #7) HB manufacture. Late 19th cent. (Musée des Faienceries de Quimper.)

Rouen

The origins of faience in Rouen date back to the building of Renaissance châteaux in the area. In the 1520 - 1530s Masseot Abaquesne, a glazer from Cherbourg designed the floor and mural tiles for the châteaux de Madrid, de la Fère-en-Tardenois, the chapel d'Anoncourt, etc. His most reknowned works are the tile flooring made for Anne de Montmorency, Connetable de France at the Château d'Ecouen (Val d'Oise) which can be seen today.

When Abaquesne died in 1564, his son, Laurens, carried on the work until 1570. From then, it was almost eighty years until the rebirth of faience making in Rouen.

In 1645, letters patent were issued to Le Sieur Granval, "to make all kinds of *faience blanche,* covered with colored enamel for public consumption". He chose Edmé Poterat to install his manufacture in the St. Sever quarter. Poterat had a monopoly on faience production for fifty years. As there were no other faienciers in the area, he called the best potters from Nevers. His factory flourished under the protection of the Sieur Granval and the king; orders for busts, vases and tiles came to furnish the Trianon de Porcelaine, built in 1670.

By 1673, Poterat's two sons had opened factories of their own. Workers came from Holland bringing examples of the Chinese decoration which had come west through the Dutch East India Company. Artists who had formerly worked at Nevers were also familiar with the oriental designs. The range of production at Rouen began to expand into a number of new artistic expressions. The following are highlights of this expansion.

The First Period

Originally commissioned to made *faience blanche,* Poterat's faienceries produced wares covered with a white, milky glaze on which blue and yellow designs were made. Occasionally the colors were brought close together to allow a green mix to occur on the edges of the design. The style was very italianate, in the tradition of Faenza.

The Chinese Influence (1660 - 1730)

After the success Delft and Nevers had enjoyed with the Hollando-Chinese designs, Rouen began to use these themes with new imagination. The Rouen interpretations became a new French style, incorporating tendrils and lambrequins into the monochrome design.

10. Rouen Large Platter, Lambrequin decoration. 18th cent. (Courtesy C. Massin, Les Faïences de Rouen)

The lambrequin, a basic decoration of the Kang-Hi period (1622 - 1722) in China was immediately successful in France and adopted by artists for different types of materials. Jean Bérain, set designer to the King, used these lines for theatrical productions; Boule, the royal cabinetmaker, used them in his marquetry work; leather, fabric and silver workers picked up the patterns; even gardeners laid out plantings in lambrequin designs.

Original Rouen Decorations

A L'Ocre Niellé Around 1725, a Rouen potter, Paul Caussy, grandfather to the Caussy who went to Quimper, designed a new motif based on the visual effect of inlaid enamel work. With swirling arabesques which formed a thick network around figures or designs in reserve, this new decoration imitated principles of marquetry or jewelry making. The underlying color was most often a yellow ocre, overpainted with black tracery.

11. Rouen Pitcher in the shape of a helmet showing the *Niellé* decoration. 18th cent. (Courtesy C. Massin, Les Faïences de Rouen)

Ferroneries Another design from Rouen was based on metal work and grilles in which the lambrequin ornamentation was curved and worked into floral motifs.

Faiences Historiées A renewed interest in mythological themes emerged around 1730. Large plaques and platters, painted by Claude Borne, Pierre Chapelle and Leleu date from this period.

Style Chinois At the same time (c. 1730) the *famille verte* of the Kang-Hi period became very popular in the West. The Rouen artist, Guillibaud, attempted to interpret Chinese designs on Rouen forms. Because the *grand feu* method could not duplicate the coloring of the Chinese products (kaolin and the *petit feu* method had not yet been discovered in the West) Guillibaud developed an original type of decoration — Oriental in feeling, but French in coloration and application. These designs included pagodas, pomegranates, bat wings, winged dragons, peacocks, oriental ducks, etc. which were modified to fit the plates, pitchers, pots and other wares, the molds of which were already available among the Rouen creations.

12. Rouen Cider pitcher decorated in the *Ferronnerie* style resembling ironwork. 18th cent. (Courtesy C. Massin, Les Faïences de Rouen)

Style Rocaille The Rouen styles, bound up to this point in the rigidity of iron work *(ferronerie)* and the *style rayonnant,* in which the pattern remained perfectly balanced and static, changed in the 1750s to a new feeling of freedom and release. The patterns became asymetrical; they seemed often to be sprinkled over the surfaces rather than geometrically placed. The forms themselves developed swirls and extra flanges, offcenter, which gave movement and vitality to the pieces. This rococo style became very popular; it is the one most often copied in the faience reproductions of the late 19th and early 20th centuries.

The Rouen painter, Dieul, who initiated this type of work, became famous for his decorations *"au carquois"* (the quiver), *"a la corne tronquée"* (foreshortened cone), *"corne d'abondance"* (cornucopia), *"paniers fleuris"* (flower baskets) and *"oeillet de Rouen"* (Rouen carnation).

13. Rouen Plate. This example illustrates the union of Chinese themes with western forms which developed into the *style rocaille.* (Courtesy of C. Massin, Les Faïences de Rouen)

This rococo style continued in Rouen until 1770 when the faience makers began to encounter difficulties securing the tin and the firewood necessary for their work.

Rouen contributed many advances in design and interpretation to the art of French faience. Perhaps one of the most important was the discovery of the red pigment which could be used in the *grand feu* method. Known to the Turks, and seen in their faience of *Iznik,* the red color was called Armenian bole. But the western faienciers had been unable to capture the secret until the Rouen painter, Denis Dorio, in 1708, wrote that he had discovered the process. Though the evidence surrounding the discovery is flawed, it is certain that the Guillibaud factory used the red in certain decorations of the early 18th century. The process was as follows: The red was usually applied after the other colors had been fired. Added as a complement to the blue designs, the gummy pigment was laid on rather thickly in lines or short strokes. It was then subjected to a supplementary firing. Always a difficult color to achieve, the red often turned brown, bubbled, or flaked off. To prevent this happening, the artists confined its use to accents rather than to large surface treatments.

Summary

In 1645 Poterat had begun his faiencerie. Protected by a fifty year monopoly, it continued under his sons' direction until the turn of the century. Then other faienceries opened in Rouen. In 1725, thirteen faienceries were listed as employers of 359 workers. In 1761, there were 570 faienciers of which 95 were specifically painters. Twenty-five furnaces were in operation. Rouen faience was sold all over France and Europe.

By the beginning of the 18th century, competition from the other potting centers began to cut into Rouen's trade. At the same time there existed a growing shortage of forests in the Rouen area for which the faience makers had to compete with iron smiths and numerous other tradesmen who used wood for fuel. In addition, the problem of procuring good tin became more severe. Tin from England was cut off because of the wars; tin from Germany had many impurities which required a longer and more difficult process of preparation.

By the end of the 18th century, at the time of the Revolution, only one or two factories remained active. In 1802, under Napoleon, six other factories opened briefly. By 1847 the last factory in Rouen had closed down.

Rouen Marks

Rouen marks are rare on the early pieces, with the exception of some Edmé Poterat examples. Later signatures indicate individual painters rather than particular factories. Many of the initials attributed to Rouen are unidentified. Most *bibelots,* or small collectibles available today which are marked Rouen are later reproductions whose mark refers to the type of decoration, not the town of origin.

Moustiers Marseilles

High in the mountains of the *Basses Alpes* region seems an unlikely birthplace for one of the greatest French faiences of the 18th century; but it was here in Moustiers that the Clérissy dynasty began, nurtured by a proximity to Italy, the exchange of travelers, workmen and information that favored the development of the faience center.

Tradition has it that Antoine Clérissy, whose house was next door to the Servite convent, learned the secret of faience from one of the Italian monks of the order. Whether or not the tale is true, Clérissy established a faiencerie which continued its celebrated production for four generations. At Antoine's death in 1679, his two sons, Pierre and Joseph, continued the faience tradition. Pierre made the family name famous in Moustiers. He was followed by his son, Antoine II and grandson, Pierre II. The other brother, Joseph, left for Marseilles and started his own establishment in neighboring St. Jean-du-Désert. The development of *grand feu* faience in these two towns ran parallel for the next fifty years.

14. **Moustiers** Oval platter showing tiger hunt. Circa 1720. (Courtesy C. Massin, Reconnaître les Origines des Faïences Françaises)

First Period (1670 - 1730)

The styles associated with the Pierre Clérissy factory reflected strong Italian influences. Though the molds were taken from silversmiths' models of the period, decorations resembled the Nevers and Rouen translations of the Italian designs. As in Nevers, Moustiers used the cameo blue technique of blue monochrome drawing. Many of Antoine Tempesta's scenes of the hunt (mythological renditions of lion, stag, bear or ostrich hunting) were thus depicted. Other compositions included: copies of Flemish works of the 16th century;

Bible illustrations from the 17th century; heraldic designs which appeared after the publication of armorial collections at the end of the 17th century. Lambrequins from the designs of Rouen entered the Moustiers repertoire, though the details of this pattern developed into a more embroidered look and then to a lacy expression which became particular to Moustiers.

The Moustiers *pâte* was finer and lighter in weight than that of Nevers or Rouen; the glaze brighter and smoother. As time passed, Moustiers decorations took on more of their own feeling, though many of the same designs were being produced at Rouen and Nevers during this same period. Inspired by Ovid's Metamorphoses and the Labors of Hercules, Clérissy produced large platters with mythological scenes. Griffons and animal heads appeared as handles and finials.

Lastly, the publication of Bérain's engravings which stimulated the *décor Bérain* at Rouen led to the creation of a style and composition that was Moustiers' finest contribution to faience. As Giacomotti says, "the *décor Bérain* was to Moustiers what the *décor rayonnant* was to Rouen — one of the most perfect achievements of French ceramic art."

Second Period (1730 - 1790)

The second great period of Moustiers faience arose out of the workshops of Olerys and Laugier. The Olerys family of faienciers in Marseilles served their apprenticeships at Moustiers. Joseph, the patriarch, born in 1697, probably trained under the great Pierre Clérissy.

In 1723, Olerys returned to Marseilles after his sojourn in Moustiers. Three years later, at the age of twenty-nine, he was called to Alcora, Spain, where the duc d'Aranda had established a new faiencerie. As director of the production, Olerys came into contact with and was greatly influenced by the local Spanish colors and techniques. When he returned to Moustiers, he joined with his brother-in-law, Emile Laugier, to form a new factory. The Olerys - Laugier company produced a type of polychrome based on the techniques Olerys had learned in Alcora. One of these newly acquired skills was to fire the white glaze before applying the colors. The lines of the painting consequently remained thin and delicate.

The factory at Moustiers made dinner services with innovative designs including: a garland and medallion pattern based on the *style Bérain*; a pattern of rococo shell borders; a design with flag motifs called *"aux drapeaux"*, or *"à la fanfare"*; and a particularly distinctive décor *"grotesques"*. This last pattern, featuring figures of deformed proportions derived from Roman times, but had been lately revived by the publication of Jacques Callot's engravings.

Callot (1592 - 1635) was a famous engraver; born in Nancy in Lorraine, he studied art and drawing in Italy. During his Florentine period, Callot made several series of drawings on the *Commedia dell'arte* and the local street performers. The *Gubbi* were a troupe of deformed dwarfs who performed each year in Florence. These grotesque figures became popular in the 18th century as subjects for statuettes in gold and porcelain.

Olerys adopted the theme and carried the design further to include exaggerated birds and animals. The fantastic half human, half animal figures introduced in this period were painted in two colors: green and yellow; green and manganese; green and blue. Some forms were done in monochrome: yellow, manganese or green. The figures were often encircled by vegetation which resembled the potato plant, but which was probably intended to be nightshade or bittersweet.

15. **Moustiers** Covered pot, 5" tall, *décor grotesque.* Note floral finial and handles made to resemble twisted onion stalks. (Private Collection)

During this period (1739 - 1749), Jean-Etienne Baron, Jean François Pelloquin, Baptiste Solomé and Joseph Fouque joined the faiencerie. At Olerys' death in 1749, the factory began to go downhill, despite the efforts of his son to continue. The Olerys - Laugier factory closed down altogether in 1790.

By mid-century (1750) there had been in Moustiers twelve faienceries of record, employing eighty faience workers. Fouque and Pelloquin, from the Olerys factory had started up their own faiencerie in 1748. In 1783, Fouque split with Pelloquin and bought up the Pierre Clérissy factory. This marked the end of the Clérissy line in Moustiers. Fouque's son continued the production until 1852.

In 1779 Gaspard Feraud, a worker in the Fouque factory, started his own establishment. He married Catherine Ferrat whose brothers ran another factory. The Ferrat brothers managed their establishment until 1791; then the descendents of one brother, Jean-Baptiste II, kept it going until the middle of the 19th century when it is generally agreed that the *grand feu* faience production had died out in Moustiers—not to be revived until the 1930s.

It is difficult to discuss the *grand feu* faience in Moustiers without involving the production of Marseilles, because here too the Clérissy and Viry families made important contributions to faience. The earliest factories in Marseilles employed potters from Nevers and Moustiers, among the most reknowned in the *grand feu* tradition were Joseph Clérissy, Pelletier, Fauchier and Leroy.

In 1679, at his father's death, Joseph Clérissy left Moustiers for Marseilles. He bought a faiencerie in the suburbs of Marseilles, St. Jean-du-Désert and engaged two brothers Viry, painters from Moustiers. Their father and another brother worked in the Pierre Clérissy factory at Moustiers. With this obvious connection, the products of Joseph Clérissy in Marseilles and Pierre Clérissy in Moustiers were so alike that they are frequently confused today. Wandering merchants took the Moustiers wares to Aix, Avignon, Arles, Marseilles, Paris, Lyons and Grenoble. From the port of Marseilles, the fine pieces went to the Antilles, Alicante, Cadiz, Brest and St. Malo.

Unfortunately, Joseph died at a young age in 1685. His widow married the painter, François Viry and together they continued the management of the factory. When Viry died in 1697, Antoine Clérissy, the eldest son of the widow and her first husband, Joseph, took over the direction. His family maintained the production until 1733, when it passed into the Joliette family, also faienciers from Marseilles.

Meanwhile, Anne Clérissy, Joseph's daughter, married a faiencier, Etienne Heraud. When she died in 1711, she left the ownership of the Heraud factory to her daughter, Madeleine, but the direction of the work to Joseph Fauchier. From Fauchier Madeleine learned the basic technical aspects of faience making; she in turn taught her son, Louis Leroy.

Fauchier left the Heraud establishment about 1724 and started his own factory (Pantagone).

When Madeleine died in 1749, her son, Louis Leroy, established his own faiencerie at Porte du Paradis.

1750 became an important date in the history of faience in Marseilles because it was at this time that the *petit feu* method found its way to this city. Sometime in 1748 - 49 Paul Hannong, faiencier in Strasbourg, learned the secret of German hard paste porcelain; shortly afterwards came the development of *petit feu* faience. The discovery spread quickly from Strasbourg and Lunéville to Moustiers where the Ferrat brothers adopted the technique and passed it on to Marseilles.

From 1750 on, Marseilles' faience became known for its glorious coloration and extremely delicate painting. Most famous for this type of production was the faiencerie of Claude Perrin's widow, Pierrette Caudelot. Veuve Perrin, who signed her work VP ran the factory and produced exceptionally fine work from 1748 to her death in 1793.

The faienciers of the *petit feu* method paid little attention to the forms of their pieces, using available rococo molds, urns and large tureens with animal heads or fruit handles. Mostly the artists were concerned with colors and fine detail, which appeared in Chinese scenes, landscapes and farmyards replete with shepherds and their animals. The delicate drawing of flowers and fish was made possible by the discovery of "purple of Cassius", a deep crimson made by dissolving a gold coin in nitric acid and sal ammoniac. Invented by Cassius of Leyden in the 17th century, the technique traveled to China where it was used in the *famille rose* creations, returned to Meissen and the German faienceries before it spread to Strasbourg, thence to Marseilles.

Also important was the development of a transparent green enamel used as a wash over black outlines. Created during his partnership with Veuve Perrin, Honoré Savy claimed this as his invention. In any case, the addition of these two colors enabled the painters to decorate pottery as intricately as a canvas and contributed to the very high standards of painting in the Marseilles' factories.

Strasbourg

One hundred years after the first establishment at Nevers, and fifty years after Rouen, the eastern faience centers of Strasbourg, Lunéville and St. Clément entered the faience making field. The first factory, founded by Charles-François Hannong in 1721 copied Rouen's *style rayonnant* and the Chinese designs. His son, Paul-Antoine, who directed the factory from 1739 - 1760 added new colors: yellow, two shades of green and a brick red to the basic blue of the *grand feu* palette.

It is due to the leadership and creativity of Paul Hannong that Strasbourg owes its enviable reputation. Under his direction the Strasbourg factory experienced its greatest achievements. His experimentations and technical discoveries would influence all European faience making from then on. Sometime in 1744, in the course of his experiments, Paul hit upon a technique which approximated the *petit feu* method, as yet unknown in France. A piece of ceramic presented to Louis XV on his travels through Strasbourg in 1744 reveals the use of gold detail not possible on usual *grand feu* products.

Poised as it was on the German border, Strasbourg most often looked toward the East for inspiration in the arts. Leading the ceramic field at the moment was the famous, delicate porcelain of the Meissen factory. In 1748 - 49, three Lowenfinck brothers and one of their wives, all of whom had been trained at Meissen as porcelain painters settled in Strasbourg. From their experience and the aide of other German immigrants, Paul Hannong developed the *petit feu* method and muffle kiln which enabled him to use crimsons, pinks, roses and gold in the decoration of his faience. He was the first faiencier in France to use this technique and through his work the method traveled to Marseilles, Sceaux, Lunéville, Niderviller, etc. whose factories went on to specialize in this porcelain-like product.

Whether it was due to the later start in faience making, a start which caught the rococo style in full swing; or whether it was due to the exuberant German influence so prevalent in the area of Strasbourg, this faience never passed through the naive stage. Instead, it launched right away into the refined, elegant, curvaceous style, with swirls of color and naturalistic flowers that characterize Strasbourg faience.

16. Strasbourg Plate decorated in the style "German flowers", Hannong factory. (Courtesy C. Massin, Reconnaître les Origines des Faïences Françaises)

Some of the flowers were drawn on the plates with black outlines and painted with simple-graded washes. These were the ordinary ware, easily produced for the mass market. The extraordinary production has very delicate shading and artistic modeling. The "purple of Cassius", made from dissolved gold, is readily identified with classic Strasbourg. Other *petit feu* colors include a light green, a strong yellow, a violet and a brown.

In 1760, at Paul Hannong's death, his son, Joseph, took over the production. Rash speculation and financial reverses forced the closing of the factory in 1780. Though Strasbourg faience itself was finished, its reputation lived on. Many other European factories in Germany, Hungary, Sweden, and Switzerland imitated and perpetuated the style. To this day the Strasbourg designs are being duplicated by modern factories, though none of them operates in the city of Strasbourg.

Decline of French Faience

Throughout the 18th century, the faience business was threatened by economic and political factors. Basically a creation for the rich, it enjoyed great prosperity when the king called in the silver and gold to pay for his wars; then the nobles replaced their tableware with faience. But eventually declining supplies of firewood in the important areas, the inability to procure tin for the process, the long training period required for painters which was interrupted by wars and dislocations, began to erode the greatness of the big faience centers — the so-called *Cinq Grands.* The final blow, however, came in the form of the Treaty of 1786, which allowed the English creamware to invade the French market and undersell French faience. Next, English potters crossed the Channel, established factories of their own in France at Creil, Croissy, Montereau, etc. to make their popular *faïence fine.* This gave the *coup de grâce* to the ailing *grand feu* industry. Attempts on the part of several of the faienceries to alter their methods, imitate porcelain and thus compete with the English factories, for the most part failed.

By the end of the 18th century, the Strasbourg and Marseilles factories had closed down. By the middle of the 19th century Rouen was finished and Nevers production was reduced to one small factory. Of the five great original faience centers only offshoots survived. These retained their viability for one of two reasons: they were isolated and therefore relatively unaffected by the major economic and political conflicts; or else they had resumed making plain, utilitarian ware for local consumption, relying on the trade of the common people rather than on the fickle whims of the rich and royal who no longer ordered fancy embellishments for their castles and estates.

The period of 1789 - 1815, which encompasses the years of the French Revolution, the foreign wars, Napoleon's Blockade and finally his defeat at Waterloo, proved devastating to the French economy and by extension to the production of French faience. As it had been known in the 18th century, this celebrated art form was particularly desired by and designed for the nobles and rich bourgeoisie who could indulge themselves with luxury items. Times had changed. Castles had been destroyed or taken over by the state. Nobles returned penniless as *emigrés.* Luxury items gave way to necessities. It was not until the 1830s and 40s that new forces operating in the society and in the economy would bring renewed interest in faience making in the old tradition.

PART II

Faience in the Age of Industrialization

Grand Feu:

- **Quimper**
- **Boulogne-sur-Mer**
- **Desvres**
- **Malicorne**
- **Blois**
- **Angoulème**

Faienceries of the East: Petit Feu Tradition

- **Lunéville and St. Clément**
- **Sarreguemines**

Conclusion

- **CA**

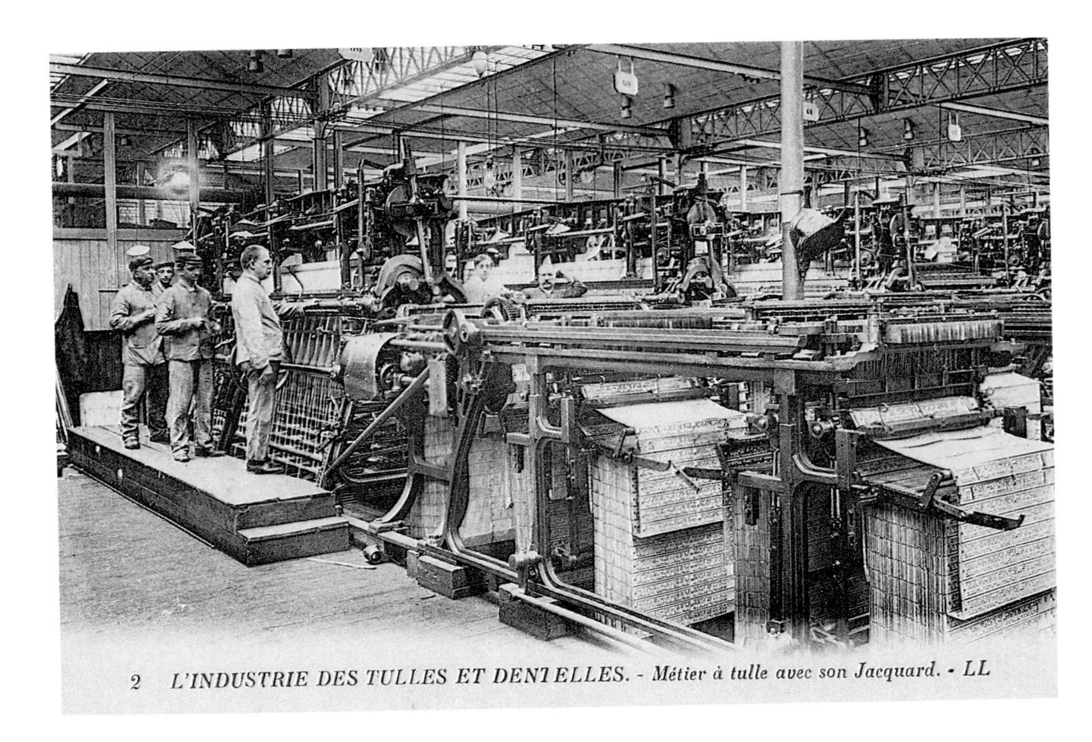

17. Old post card showing the interior of a lace factory. Late 19th cent.

18. Old post card showing vacationers and bathers at the popular seaside resort, Boulogne-sur-Mer. Early 20th cent.

Faience in the Age of Industrialization

Though the contemporary concepts of individual liberty, popular sovereignty and national patriotism arose from the ideals of the French Revolution and were spread throughout Europe by Napoleon and the events of the Metternich era, it would not have been possible for democratic civilization to have prospered without the effects of the Industrial Revolution. This revolution, or more properly, evolution, for it took place gradually over many years, profoundly affected the work place, the life style and the mobility, both social and physical, of ordinary people.

The Industrial Revolution began in England, which seems surprising at first since France was the leading European country in the 18th century. Her industry and trade were superior to England's at least up to the dawn of the French Revolution. In 1785, she had three times the population of England, greater markets for her wares, raw materials and rich natural resources. However, France's industrial development was hampered by a number of particular conditions. First, as a country of small-scale agriculture, small communities and small shops, France's long tradition of handwork and fine luxury production was valuable commercially, but not suited to be converted to machine. Secondly, her markets reduced by Napoleon's wars and confined by the blockade did not encourage large-scale manufacture which would have made the use of machines profitable. Thirdly, France lacked the capital for investing in industrial experimentation. The deficiency of the banking system, the bankruptcy of the government and the unproductive use of accumulated wealth precluded most capitalistic ventures. It was not until 1830, when the July Revolution dethroned aristocratic, old régime Charles X and replaced him with a "bourgeois king", Louis Philippe, that a shift in political, social and economic philosophy could emerge.

Fostering industry and the importation of English machinery and techniques, the régime of Louis Philippe encouraged free trade, private initiative and capitalistic investment. Though industry in France was small and lagged behind the achievements in England, changes began to occur. In 1840 power-driven machines were introduced to the French textile industries. In 1842, the first railroad between Paris and Rouen, thence to Le Havre was built. In the 1850s and 60s, the railroad extended from Paris to Strasbourg, Lyons, Marseilles, Brest, Bordeaux and Toulouse.

In France, as throughout Europe, the winds of liberalism began to blow. This new feeling for individualism led to changes in the old class structure; it broke down traditional social and commercial barriers; it encouraged public education and the extention of public works. A new bourgeoisie emerged, composed of trained government functionaries, wealthy factory owners and an enriched middle class.

With the increased wealth and education came also a widening interest in past glories. 1830 - 1878 was a period noted for the expansion of public art galleries, the opening of national museums, international expositions and the creation of public monuments. The period was Romantic, characterized by sentimentality, drama and ornamentation.

During this same period, improved communication, trade and travel furthered curiosity in the field of household arts, furniture and art objects. Travelers now brought home "what-nots" from far away to put into their "curio cabinets", souvenirs of their trips and knick-knacks for their shelves. Thus a new market was being created for souvenir items, fantasy products and decorative pieces supported by vacationers and gift-givers from the class of the *nouveau riche.*

In the area of faience making this new wave became very evident. Faience in the age of industrialization, by necessity became a different product from that of the 18th century. In 1830, a document by Bastenaire-Daudenart, Art de Fabriquer la Faience Blanche recouverts d'un Email transparent, listed the problems of the old tin-glaze, *grand feu* method and recommended the production of the practical English dinnerware. The dawn of the factory method had come. Machines were available to form molds, blend clays and glazes, expedite the work. Designs could now be printed and applied quickly by workers who did not need to spend long years learning the painters' art. Items could now be made cheaply, in a series. The article pointed out clearly that the industrial age had taken over the artistic province and that economy, uniformity and speed of production must become the new goals of the faienciers. Nor could these budding industrialists ignore the facts that coal was available and more economical to use than wood; that modern kilns could be regulated so fewer failures occured in the firing cycles; that molds and standardization of models allowed for more production at a lower cost. Gradually research in chemistry led also to improvements in the composition of the clays. Toxicity in the lead glazes, the cause of saturnism, that dread disease of the old faience workers, could be eliminated.

In response to the pressures of industrialization and all of the obvious advantages provided by technical progress, French faience developed along two lines: 1) *faïence fine* with mechanical decoration; and 2) a revitalized version of the traditional faience *(grand feu* method) with hand painting.

Faïence fine was essentially a British import. Arriving on the French scene as a result of the Treaty of 1786, the process hastened the demise of the already ailing traditional faience and royal porcelain factories.

Relatively cheap to produce, the product lent itself well to decoration by stencil and printed reproduction. This printed decoration was also a British technique, introduced in France by Potter, who bought the Chantilly factory in 1792. Potter's process preceded decalcomania, which was developed by the Germans a decade or so later.

With the invention of printed reproductions on a ceramic base, innumerable possibilities for decoration opened up. Famous paintings were made into transfers; songs, sayings, anecdotes, historical events, fables, moral dicta, scenes, monuments and on and on brought history, culture, manners, politics and propaganda into everyone's dining room. *Faïence fine* became the "democratic dishware" which appealed to and instructed the collector/ buyer of modest means.

Three great centers of *faïence fine* were: Montereau, Creil and Gien. A very brief history of each follows.

Creil - Montereau

The factory at Montereau, 80 kilometers southeast of Paris was founded in 1748. Directed by a series of Englishmen: the Garvey brothers, Jean Holker, the Clarks and Jean Hill, the Montereau firm was sold in 1819 to the owner of the Creil works.

The Creil faiencerie, located on the estate of the Prince de Condé, 60 kilometers north of Paris, had been founded in 1796 by St. Cricq-Cazaux. Five or six years later, an Englishman, Bagnall, left the faiencerie at Chantilly to work at Creil. Here he trained thirty workers in the production of *faïence fine.* Their success was immediate. Montereau was joined to Creil in 1819 and they stayed together for seven years. During this time both firms continued to produce and to sign their own names to their products. In 1825, St. Cricq sold the Montereau factory to Messers Lebeuf and Thibaut. In 1840, Lebeuf and his new associate, Millet, joined the Creil-Montereau firms again. The Creil studios shut down in 1895, but the name Creil-Montereau was retained until 1955, when the company's assets were liquidated.

At first, the production of Creil and Montereau was classic *faïence fine,* a combination of *argile,* a white fire clay and sand. Around 1834, the clay was changed to *porcelaine opaque, semi-porcelaine* or *terre de fer,* by the inclusion of feldspar and kaolin. As the new ingredients and refinements were added to the composition of the clay, the names were changed to "petrocerame" in 1844 and "kaolina" in 1867. The glazes were also improved from having a high percentage of lead to finally having no lead at all in the mix.

Gien

The products of the Gien factory belong to both the *faïence fine* and the traditional faience categories. Founded in 1821 by Hall in the old convent of the Minimes on the banks of the Loire, the factory continues to produce at that spot today.

Hall had been the owner of the Montereau factory at the time of its sale to Creil. By the terms of his sales contract, he agreed not to start a competing firm within a certain distance of his former factory. At Gien he found an ideal location.

Over the years Gien has produced a full gamut of ware — utilitarian to decorative, special orders for impressive occasions to little objects for collectors. Inspired by the prestigious faience of the 17th and 18th centuries, Gien has copied Rouen, Moustiers, Marseilles, La Rochelle, Delft, Italian majolica, Longwy, and Wedgwood, among others. Gien has made its own interpretations of encrusted faience — Palissy-type ware, armorial reproductions and Callot designs. Most well-known to American collectors is Gien's classic Italian style which resembles Blois work of the same period. The famous *bleu de Gien* characterizes these pieces.

Chronology

1819	Merlin Hall left Montereau.
1821	Hall founded Gien.
1822	Hall took Guyon as Associate.
1829	Guyon created a new society with de Boulen and Guerin.
1851	de Boulen and Geoffroy.
1857	S.A. (Société Anonyme) Geoffroy. Under M. Geoffroy's direction the factory prospered and the production diversified.
	Medals won at the international expositions.
1860	Gien became one of the six greatest *fabriques* in France. Manufactured reproductions of faience and series of special themes.
1870	Factory building used as an infirmary by both sides during the Franco-Prussian War.
1872	Gien restored as a faiencerie.
1880	Made tiles for the Paris Metro. By the end of the century, Gien was making every type of pattern in the repertoire of the old faience and many new designs of their own.
1984	Factory bought by Pierre Jeuffroi.
1985	Factory museum opened.
	A series of marks and their dates can be found in the Index of Marks.

While these three centers developed the production of *faïence fine* in the English tradition, other French factories in more remote areas preserved the *grand feu* method. They stimulated interest in the traditional faience and revived the production of this art form by designing new items for the popular market and by creating new collectibles for middle class patrons. Most prominent among the 19th and early 20th century *grand feu* faience centers are: Quimper, Boulogne, Desvres, Malicorne, Blois, Angoulême, St. Clément-Lunéville and Sarreguemines.

These are not the only centers of *grand feu* faience production, but they are the ones whose products appear most frequently in private collections today. A special chapter is devoted to the study of CA, a prolific factory which up to now has defied detection and identification.

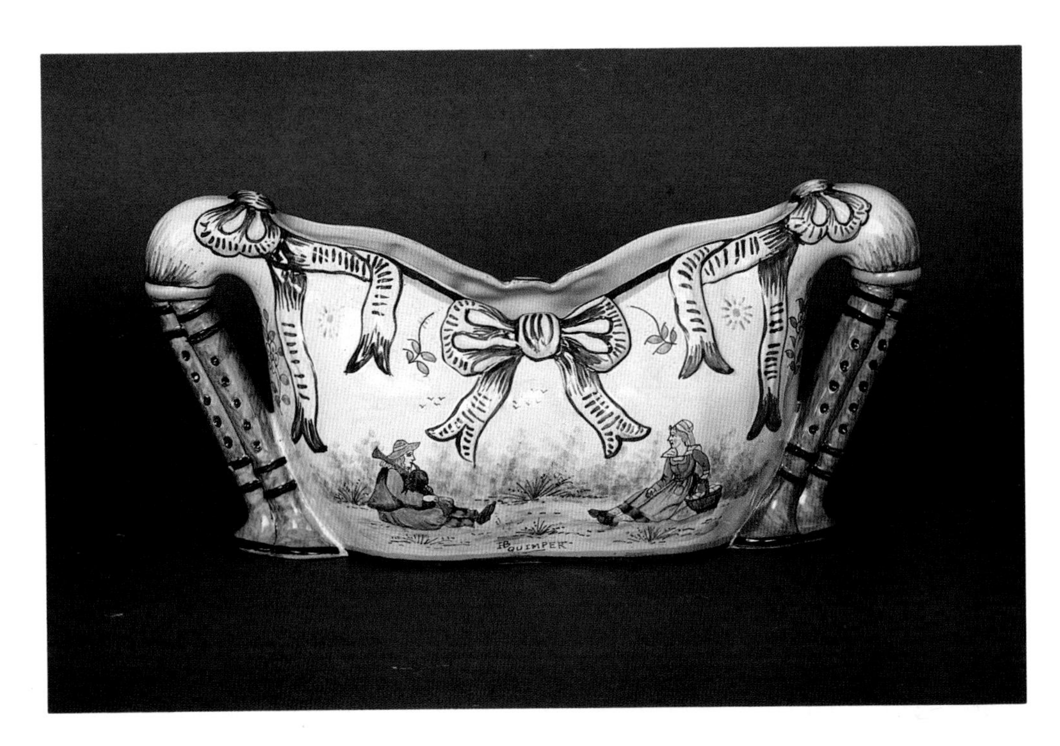

19. Quimper Jardinière 14" x 6". Double bagpipe design recalls the Breton's Celtic origins. Bagpipes and horns *(binious* and *bombardes)* are played at festivals and *Pardons.* HB factory, Mid 20th cent. (Private Collection)

20. Quimper Tray 15½" x 9¾". Breton figures are taken from Lalaisse's drawings. Border design is known as *"croisillé".* Henriot factory, 1920s. (Private Collection)

Quimper

Quimper (pronounced "camp-pair") is the chief city of the department of Finistère, located in Brittany, the province in the extreme northwest section of France. Separated in the past by distance, culture and customs (the natives are Celtic in origin) from the mainstream of France and the French economy, Quimper is one of those potting centers which managed to ride out the hard times by retreating into the local market and by adjusting to the new demands.

In tracing the history and development of the three major faienceries which date from the 18th century or earlier, we will see how Quimper ware survived the crises which destroyed the other 18th century centers and remains vital today.

Maison Bousquet - de la Hubaudière

21. Watercolor by F. Hippolyte Lalaisse Galerie Armoricaine, 1845. Inspiration for #20. Woman in festival costume and *coiffe* of Concarneau.

In 1695 Jean Baptiste Bousquet, a native of Sainte-Zacharie, near Marseilles, settled in Quimper (Loc-Maria), took over an existing pottery and, in 1690, constructed his first kilns. Raised in the traditions of Marseilles, where his name is on the factory records, Bousquet brought new ideas and energy to the Quimper pottery workshop. The original shop was soon outgrown, so he absorbed two neighboring properties. When he died, December 8, 1708, his son, Pierre Bousquet, a former worker in the Moustiers factory, took over the business.

Quimper was a good location, near centers of commerce. Wood for firing the ovens was abundant; good clay in the *Anse de Toulven* was readily available several kilometers away.

In 1731 Pierre Bousquet took his son-in-law,

22. Quimper Plate 9¼" diameter. Decoration combines the old Rouen themes: the peacock, *à la corne,* and the typical red chain border design. Henriot factory, 1920s. (Private Collection)

23. Quimper Bowl 11½" diameter. Based on the popular pseudo-Chinese English Willow pattern, this French design transforms the Mandarin's house into a church, the willow into a sponged tree with a peacock and the houseboat into a French ship. HB factory, 1930s. (Private Collection)

Pierre Bellevaux as assistant. The latter had been a turner in Nevers, which explains the introduction of the Nevers style into the faience at Quimper.

In 1739, a young man from Rouen, Pierre Clément Caussy, joined the association. A descendant of well-known potters, Pierre Clément brought with him many traditions and skills of the Rouen factories. His grandfather, Paul Caussy, had invented a vaulted oven which much improved the firing process. He also was credited with having introduced a rare yellow ocre glaze on the Rouen productions.

Pierre Clément's father, Pierre Paul Caussy, had traveled widely to Nevers, Italy, Switzerland, and Louisiana in America. He had learned all of the potting skills and could do the work of any of his employees. In 1747, Pierre Paul wrote Traité de la Faience which divulged the secrets of Rouen manufacture. Unfortunately, most of the work has been lost, but the few remaining fragments reveal the remarkable degree of detail with which Caussy recorded all the techniques.

In 1749, Pierre Clément Caussy married Bousquet's granddaughter, Marie-Jeanne Bellevaux. Later that year, at Bousquet's death, Pierre Clément took over the direction of the faiencerie. The choice of this young man (he was only thirty years old at the time) proved most advantageous to the Quimper trade. He constructed new ovens, hired more workers and artisans. He brought designs and *poncifs* (paper stencils) from Rouen and copied the successful styles of Rouen and Nevers. Because he preferred the Rouen clay, he had it transported to Quimper. Merchants came daily to buy the popular pottery which, because of its similarity in consistency and style, was hardly distinguishable from Rouen ware.

During the next thirty-three years, Pierre Clément Caussy directed the Quimper faience works with competence and skill.

In 1782, Caussy died and the business passed to his son-in-law, Antoine de la Hubaudière, husband of Marie-Elizabeth Caussy. De la Hubaudière did not direct the factory for long, however, because he became involved with the Girondin representatives to the Convention at Paris. When the Girondin government fell, de la Hubaudière became a fugitive. He was caught and killed by the Chouans on May 13, 1794. His widow, *Citoyenne* Caussy took over the direction of the factory and enlarged its production along utilitarian lines. By leaving aside the creation of highly decorated wares in the styles of Nevers and Rouen, and by concentrating on the production of ordinary plates, bowls, porringers, pots and the cheaper *grès* ware, the HB factory successfully weathered the political and economic crises.

24. Old post card showing Breton man in the costume of Douarnenez.

Clément de la Hubandière, son of Antoine and Marie-Elizabeth took over the direction of the family factory for a time; then it passed to his nephew, Félix, who was the owner from 1872 - 1882. During these years a Monsieur Fougeray filled the position of director at the factory. He was responsible for the choice of designs and the general production of the *Maison Hubaudière* . Unfortunately, Fougeray chose to continue distributing the Quimper renditions of Rouen patterns. These were extremely commonplace at the time, as many of the other faienceries were also reproducing old Rouen. A report on the Exposition of 1878 in Paris at the Champs de Mars declares à propos the HB exhibit: "Always the same. Imitation of the old Rouen taken from the worst period...While old Rouen offered such admirable models in the red and blue designs, why would a manufacturer imitate unceasingly the Rouen *à la corne*? It takes a man of little taste to buy the fakes (or to make them)."

25. Quimper Plate 9¼" diameter. Decoration taken from old post card like #24. HB factory, late 19th cent. (Private Collection)

At Félix's death in 1882, Fougeray also resigned as director. The factory was put up for sale to pay the inheritors. Félix's second wife, the former Alix-Léonie Malherbe de la Bouëscière, now his widow, bought the company and made it into a corporation known as *"Manufacture de Faïences artistiques et ordinaire, grès, poteries de la Hubaudière et Cie, fondeé à Quimper en 1685".* She also married a second time to the count Le Court de Béru.

26. Quimper Plate 9¼" diameter. Decoration taken from old post card like #27. HB factory, Early 20th cent. (Private Collection)

This is the period in which the *Grande Maison* HB produced fewer items of the Rouen type and began to enlarge the scope and production of the Breton themes.

Guy de la Hubaudière, son of Félix and Alix was the last of the Hubaudière line. He died in the First World War on August 31, 1916. The factory, which had not been producing for a while was bought in 1917 by a fellow faiencier, Jules Verlingue, from Boulogne-sur-Mer.

Maison Eloury - Porquier

27. Old post card showing Breton woman in the costume of Ploudiry.

At about the time of Marie-Elizabeth Caussy's marriage to Antoine de la Hubaudière (1772), other events were taking place which would influence the manufacture of Quimper faience. François Eloury, a worker in the Caussy (Bousquet) firm emerged as a master potter. Fifteen years later, in 1787, he is mentioned in the civil register as Master of a faience factory in Quimper (Loc-Maria).

After the Revolution, the Eloury factory passed from François to his son, Guillaume. As none of his sons was interested in the business, Guillaume Eloury took his son-in-law, Charles Porquier, as assistant and successor. Charles Porquier who had married Hélène Thérèse Eloury in 1809, came from a potting center in Limagne, Auvergne. His successors were his sons, Charles and Clet-Adolphe Porquier. The latter was born in 1813 and died in 1869. His widow, the former Augustine Carof, took direction of the factory at her husband's death. She took as her associate Alfred Beau, a photographer and an easel painter.

Beau, who arrived in Quimper around 1870, had first approached the HB factory with his designs and examples. Apparently Fougeray did not wish to allow Beau to sign his work along with the HB mark; Beau turned to Mme. Porquier's establishment.

With the arrival of Alfred Beau a new department of artistic faience was created at the Porquier factory. Taking his theme from the increasing interest in local traditions, folklore, customs and costumes, Beau designed a vaste series of country scenes: over 200 different renderings of wedding processions, dancers, pipers, children playing, farmers resting, bowling on the ground, fishermen, beggars, grandparents telling stories to their grandchildren, etc. many with *décor riche* borders. This leafy design done in blue, or green with a shield of Quimper or Brittany at the top of the piece, became a copyrighted decoration belonging to the Porquier establishment.

28. Quimper Fountain. Green *décor riche* design surrounding Beau's Breton scenes. Reservoir: 14" tall (minus dolphin crown and lid). Taproom scene, called *Pleyben,* shows barrel with AB initials for Alfred Beau. Basin: 14" x 6". Scene of a mother and child; area not indicated. Porquier factory, Late 19th cent. (Private Collection)

29. Quimper Platter 21¼" x 16". Border of chimera surrounding Nevers' style decoration. Porquier factory: signed ♇. This is one of the earliest designs of the association, predating Beau's Breton scenes, 1870s. (Private Collection)

30. Quimper Plate *"Légende Bretonne"*
Marked: Quimper. Henriot reissue, Early 20th cent.

Alfred Beau was a native Breton, born in Morlaix and married to the daughter of Emile Souvestre, also a Morlaix native. Influenced by his father-in-law's works, Les Derniers Bretons (four volumes 1835 - 1837) and Foyer Breton (1844) which described the folklore and flavor of Brittany in story form, Beau created the country scenes and a collection of *"Légendes Bretonnes"* which celebrated the Celtic wit and whimsy. Among these *"légende"* pieces, which show the folk beliefs and superstitions are some titled: Le Diable devenu Recteur, Yan Coz chez les diables, Le biniou et les korrigans and Le diable trompé.

31. Quimper Plate *"Légende Bretonne"*
Marked: Quimper Henriot reissue, Early 20th cent.

Beau also created a series known as *"botanique"*. Made in several molds, the plates are of a bluish-gray cast, characteristically banded in yellow. The decorations include flowers, fruits, birds, insects, fish, small animals and flowering shrubs. According to Roullot, there were about fifty different designs in each of the series. The florals are large and lifelike, laid over the entire plate. Their delicate coloring and detail make them choice collectors items today.

The series of folk scenes, the *légendes bretonnes* and the *botaniques* which were created in the period of Beau's association with Mme. Porquier's firm (1872 - 1903) bear their combined signatures. The mark is:

32. Quimper Plate *"Botanique"*
Marked: Late 19th cent.

From 1890 on, despite the success of their production, the Porquier factory sustained great financial difficulties. The association was dissolved and Alfred Beau left Quimper for Cancale in 1903. The owner's son, Arthur Porquier, reissued the AP signature on small items — this mark had been used sporadically by the father some twenty years before.

In 1905, the factory closed. Several years later, around 1913, the marks and models were legally purchased by the Henriot firm who produced the

Porquier-Beau designs again. The following signature was used on these reissues from around 1918 - 1930.

HB QUIMPER

Maison Dumaine - Tanquerey - Henriot

In 1778, Guillaume Dumaine, a descendant of potters in Normandy since 1422, set up another factory in Quimper. The production of this factory was mainly *grès* ware, utilitarian in nature with very simple decoration.

When Guillaume died in 1821, his son, also Guillaume, took over the direction until 1858. In that year Marie-Renée, granddaughter of the first Guillaume, and now married to Jean-Baptiste Tanquerey, inherited the business. Her husband was the director. An inventory done at the time (1860) indicates that the factory was quite small. It operated two ovens; one for *grès,* one for faience, and employed only five people. No trademark or signature has been recorded of the Maison Tanquerey.

33. **Quimper** Plate *"Botanique"* 9¼" diameter. Seahorse with fronds. Marked and impressed: HB , Late 19th cent. (Private Collection)

In 1864, Marie-Augustine Tanquerey married Pierre-Jules Henriot who was associated with his father-in-law's firm. At Tanquerey's death, his three children inherited the factory, though it appears that Marie-Augustine and Pierre-Jules were the primary directors. At Pierre-Jules' death in 1884, his son, Jules Henriot, only eighteen years old at the time, became the sole director of the Tanquerey-Henriot establishment.

The years 1882 - 1890 were very hard economically all over France. The crash of 1882 created a migration of country people to the cities in search of jobs. The shortage of personal spending money reduced the demand for luxury goods.

In 1895 the Trades Union Congress was formed; it grew into the Syndicalist organization on a national scale. This movement used strikes to break the power of the capitalist owners of factories. Their aim was to build a syndicalistic society. From 1906 - 1911 industrial unrest provoked strikes in all areas; among the electricians, the building and food industry workers, the navy, and the vinegrowers. In 1910, a general strike was called on the railway.

As we have seen, the early years of the 20th century were not favorable to the Porquier firm. Finances at the HB factory were also in trouble. Records in the archives of the Quimper faiencеries show that the factory was unable to pay its employees and its creditors. In April, 1905, twenty-four HB workers went out on strike. In 1906, at Mme. de Béru's death, the factory went up for sale to pay the heirs. Jules Henriot from the competing firm tried to acquire the HB factory at that time, but he was unsuccessful.

Under Jules Henriot, the HR factory had grown very well. Despite the crises already mentioned, Quimper products were enjoying a great popularity. The opening of the rail lines brought travelers and visitors to the far ends of Brittany. Tourists on holiday at the famous beaches of La Baule, Dinard and Perros-Guirec, among others, brought home a memento of their Breton vacation, thus spreading Quimper's reputation all over the continent.

Because of their great popularity, the faiences of Quimper began to be counterfeited and copied by other potteries in France and abroad. The flood of fakes on the market so disturbed Jules Henriot that he wrote a declaration *"De la Protection de Faïences bretonnes ou Faïences de Quimper"* in 1908. This pamphlet protests the influx of imitations from Desvres, Malicorne and Angoulême; deplores the merchants' careless disregard for authenticity, and underlines the decision of the Tribunal de Commerce de Quimper (Aug. 12, 1904) that a souvenir of Quimper must bear the signature of the place in which it was made. From that point on the products of the Henriot and the HB factories bore the added signature *Quimper.* We know, therefore, that a piece marked *HR Quimper* or *HB Quimper* was made after 1904 and belongs rightly in the 20th century.

As the Porquier factory was about to close down, this convention did not affect its wares. Later, when Jules Henriot reissued the Porquier models, he signed them

PB Quimper

Between the World Wars (1920 - 1940)

Under Jules Henriot's leadership, the Henriot factory grew to rival the HB factory - *Grande Maison.* Both factories experienced a great deal of expansion and innovation in the period between the wars. The tourist business thrived and the *petit breton* articles continued to be big sellers, but new designs were also in demand.

In 1920, Mathurin Méheut, an artist famous for his illustrations of sea life, boats, sailors and *fruits de mer,* joined the Henriot firm. His work and the inspiration of other artists rejuvenated the production of Quimper ware. Throughout the 1920s and 30s they introduced new, bold designs based on Celtic themes, or patterns taken from the traditional needlework on their heavily embroidered costumes; they stressed linear forms. Some of these artists were Géo Fourier, André Galland, Yannick and Suzanne Creston, J.E. Sévellec, Bachelet, Lionel Floch, Lenoir, Armel Beaufils, C. Maillard, Pol, R. Michaud, L.H. Nicot; Mesdames L. Vincent-Blandin, Chevalier-Kervern, J. Haffen, Anie Mouroux, Ravallec-Mazet and Mlle. Monfort.

34. Quimper Tureen lid *"Fruits de Mer"* 9½" diameter. Starfish and snail decoration from Mathurin Méheut's *"Service de Mer".* Marked: Henriot Quimper and signed MM (Private Collection)

For the Colonial Exposition in Paris in 1931, artists working for the Henriot factory created prize-winning African and Oceanic statuary. These men: Emile Monier, Gaston Broquet, René Nivelt, among others, also painted native village scenes and tropical landscapes on plates and other items for the colonial display. Today, more than fifty years later, Quimper collectors are often surprised to come upon Quimper products so totally different from the characteristic Breton folk ware.

The HB factory, which in 1917 had come under the ownership of Jules Verlingue from Boulogne, in 1922 took on a new director, Louis Bolloré. The firm then became known as *"Société Jules Verlinque, Bolloré et Cie, Etablissement de la Grande Maison HB".* Shortly thereafter, the HB factory moved across the Odet from its original site to a new location in Loc-Maria, near the Eglise de Loc-Maria. Part of this property had once belonged to the old Porquier faiencerie.

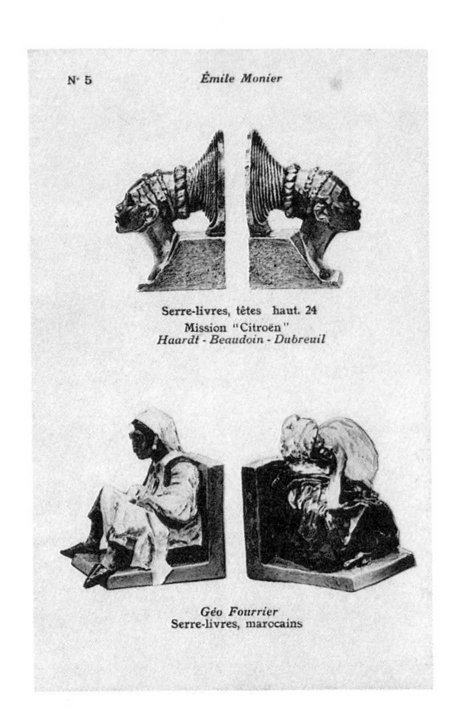

35. Old post card of Quimper statuary entered in Paris Exposition, 1925.

36. Quimper Statue of Old Woman by L.H. Nicot 8¼" tall. Henriot factory, 1930s. (Private Collection)

37. Quimper Sardine plate 9½" diameter. Advertisement for Amieux Frères sardines. The saying translates: The real sardines AMIEUX FRÈRES carry the motto—always the best. This slogan includes a pun on the manufacturer's name: AMIEUX and *mieux,* meaning the best. HB factory, Early 20th cent. (Private Collection)

The Battle of the Marks (1921 - 1922)

In 1921, Jules Henriot renewed his rights to the mark HR, which he had used since 1894, and began a law suit against the *"Société Verlingue"* for their copying of Henriot designs. He also accused the competing firm of using the *poncifs* or paper outlines which the workers had taken from his factory. The factories were only a few blocks away from each other, and the workers changed employment with regularity.

HR

In 1922, Verlingue retaliated with a counter suit in which he claimed Henriot's mark was an imitation of the HB signature. His appeal was rejected in Quimper, so he applied to the court at Rennes. The outcome of the suit required Henriot to cease using the HR mark and replace it with two letters H.R., separated by a period. Henriot never adopted this signature; instead he chose to sign the name in full, enlarging the R in the middle to remind the customer of his former mark.

HenRiot QUIMPER

During the 1920s, the HB firm also hired prominent artists to produce new designs and modern decorations. In 1922, Verlingue and Bolloré registered their mark ODETTA to be used on a new line of artistic *grès* ware. Specializing in earth colors, contrasting geometric shapes and shadowed figures, this modern expression won many medals for the HB factory. Artists who contributed to this line were: Georges Brisson, Alphonse Chanteau, Louis Garin, Marius Giot, Georges Renaud, Paul Fouillen, Rol and Beauclaire.

38. **Quimper** Pitcher 4¼" tall.
HB factory ODETTA, 1930s.
(Private Collection)

Other HB artists who specialized in sculpted animal and peasant figures were:

Kervella	large peasant dancers
Brion	large peasant figurines often old people

Berthe Savigny	babies and young children
René Quillivic	Breton figurines in everyday poses
Robin	peasant figures
Mme. A. Porson	large busts; peasant figures
Le Bozec	large peasant figures
Marius Giot	animal figures; baby with dog; mouse book-ends
Jacques Nam	cats; also some dogs; rabbits
M.L. Bar	sea birds
Rol	seal book-ends

39. Quimper Vase 12¼" tall. HB factory ODETTA, probably Fouillen. Circa 1925. (Private Collection)

At the exhibit held in Paris in 1925, L'Exposition Internationale des Arts Décoratifs et Industriels Moderns, the new artistic expressions took the name of the exposition — art déco. The ceramic entries, both in *grès* and in painted faience, demonstrated new streamlined contours, geometric patterns, sharp angles, bold curves and strident color schemes. The artists who received recognition for their work in this exhibit were: François Bazin, Bouvier, René Quillivic, François Caujan (Fanch) and Alphonse Chanteau.

40. Quimper Statue of Girl, titled *"Jeune Fille de Plouhinec"*, 15½" tall, in *grès*, by René Quillivic. HB factory, 1930s. (Private Collection)

41. Quimper Basket 7" x 4½" *Décor #9: Genre Moderne*, sometimes called Apple pattern, HB factory, 1930s. (Private Collection)

Paul Fouillen

In 1928, Paul Fouillen, former head of one of the art studios in the HB firm and prolific contributor to the ODETTA line, moved to the Place du Styvel and set up his own factory. Influenced by the Breton embroideries and the Celtic illustrations found in ancient Irish manuscripts, he created his own ceramic expression. More *grès* than faience in substance, the clay body is heavy, the decoration, bold and angular. The colors are often somber, using browns, dark greens, and maroon.

42. Quimper Teapot 4½" tall, Fouillen factory, 1930s. (Private Collection)

More popular among American collectors is the line of wooden objects: plates, small trinket boxes, trays, and small dishes on which the Breton figure or figures are carved and painted with a bright, shiny enamel.

In 1960, Maurice Fouillen took over his father's factory and continues to produce today. Though close to retirement age, Maurice works alone and has apparently made no plans for his successor.

The mark of the factory is:

On the wooden ware, the mark is:

43. Quimper Wooden plate 5¼" diameter. Figure painted in bright color; border painted to represent crackled glaze. Signed: P. Fouillen, 1940s. (Private Collection)

During the Second World War, while Brittany was occupied by the German army, the faienceries were allowed to continue operating as long as a certain amount of the production was made for the Germans. Some examples of this ware can be found today: a large, round platter picturing a German soldier surrounded by Breton motifs, signed by G. Renaud 1940, came up for auction in April 1982; a tile with the decoration of a German U Boat is in a private collection. Generally speaking, the production level was rather low because manpower and fuel were limited.

After World War II

44. Quimper Pitcher 4¼" tall, Keraluc factory. Rust colored glaze overpainted with white in rooster design, 1950s.

Keraluc

In 1946, Victor Lucas established a faiencerie in Quimper (Loc-Maria) on Mount Frugy. Having been a ceramist with Henriot for seventeen years, and then with HB for four years, Lucas decided to start his own concern: *Keraluc*. The name reflects its very Breton appeal. *Ker* means village or house, so *Keraluc* means house of Lucas. He collected local artists and promoted local designs, being careful to preserve the traditional technique and authentic Breton patterns.

For a period of time, this factory produced only *grès* ware, but recently they returned to making traditional faience, entirely hand painted and mostly all hand turned.

45. Quimper Statue of Breton couple 3½" x 5". Keraluc factory, 1950s. (Private Collection)

When Lucas died, Pol Lucas and Mme. Chauveau, his children, managed the factory. In 1985 the factory was sold to M. Beaugendre.

The mark of the factory is:

Keraluc
prés Quimper

At the HB establishment, Jules Verlingue died in 1946 and Louis Bolloré continued as director until 1952. At that point the son, Jean-Yves Verlingue took over the direction. His technical director was Louis Leonus; the production director was Jean Rouillard.

At the Henriot factory, Jules Henriot continued until 1944, when he turned over the directorship to his two sons, Robert and Joseph. These two continued together until Robert retired in 1955; his son, Alain then entered the firm, taking both the technical and managerial roles. Alain's cousin Yves also joined the firm in the early 1960s. From 1964 - 1967, the factory suffered financial reverses and the Henriot firm deteriorated dramatically. At the same time, the town of Quimper planned to widen the road to Benodet — this would go right through the Henriot buildings. A solution was achieved: the Verlingue establishment, HB, would enlarge its facility and take in the Henriot workers, numbering about 100. The joined firms, directed by a joint board of directors, would be called *"Les Faïenceries de Quimper".* This was done in 1968.

Though both factories were housed under the same roof, actually two factories were still producing. The Henriot group continued to make their designs; they were marked with an Henriot stamp and mailed to Henriot clients. In another part of the building, HB painters drew HB patterns on their products, marked their wares with an HB stamp and mailed them to HB clients.

During the years 1982 - 1983, the Quimper factories experienced months of financial difficulties, labor disputes and strikes. Twice the factory declared bankruptcy, tried to reorganize and finally was put up for sale. In January 1984, an American couple, Paul and Sarah Janssens, longtime importers of Quimper ware in the States, formed a limited company with twenty-five shareholders and bought the faiencerie.

HB Henriot
Quimper France
Peint main

The factory has remained in the same location, in the same building; however, the new firm has integrated the two former productions. Painters, many of whom were hired back, now work side by side; each learns the patterns of both HB and Henriot. The new mark reflects the union of the former competitors. Both houses are represented in the management: Bernard Verlingue, son of the previous owner is Technical Director, Pierre Henriot, son of Alain, is the new Director General.

The Remarkable Staying Power of Quimper

The question often arises — why when other more prestigious faience centers failed has Quimper managed, not only to survive, but to thrive? As we have seen, the history of the various faience factories shows there were many financial bad times. In the 1780, politics and continental wars strained many of the factories beyond endurance. The King's and Mme. de Pompadour's patronage of Sèvres porcelain put the Rouen and Nevers faience out of favor. However, the final blows were dealt in the Treaties of Commerce 1783 and 1786, when Vergennes, the Foreign Minister, allowed the cheaper English ware to overpower the French market.

Most of the faience factories tried to compete with the English imports by making a type of porcelain, or by trying to convert faience into a more sophisticated product. The attempts failed on two counts. First, the royal protection of the Sèvres factory made porcelain competition almost impossible. Secondly, the efforts to refine faience robbed the pottery of its intrinsic charm, warmth, and popular appeal. Those who would make faience into something it was not actually caused its own demise.

Quimper, on the other hand, enjoyed the benefits of being far away from the center of the action. Obedience to Pompadour's regulations and restrictions on ceramics production or coloration was mostly ignored. Furthermore, the Breton factories had always sold most of their wares to their local customers who could be counted on to buy the utilitarian pieces for everyday use. Early on, Caussy had cautioned the factory that in hard times they should avoid making elaborate pieces which required much painting and fine hand work. Instead, they should return to simple items. Throughout the revolutionary upheavals and fiscal crises, Quimper heeded Caussy's counsel.

During the first half of the nineteenth century, while the other faienceries went out of business, the de la Hubaudière (HB) and the Eloury-Porquier factories maintained a small, but constant production of bowls, plates, pitchers and religious statues in the traditional decorations with floral or geometric patterns, or with birds and roosters in naive designs. Dumaine-Tanquerey, the smallest of the three establishments, produced mostly *grès* ware which was suitable for common household items. Thus the factories were able to stay alive, thanks to the support of the local clientele. Though it must be acknowledged the artistic level of the production had fallen from its earlier achievements. It was no longer a faience of interest.

Not until the middle of the nineteenth century would Quimper rise again in importance. Then a new spirit of national pride swept across Europe; a new interest in the common man, his life, his work, his folklore and his dress came about as a part of the Romantic movement.

Out on the far end of Brittany, separated by many small rivers, valleys and hills, hundreds of individual towns had developed their own costumes and dialects. Artists, intrigued by the richness and variety of these folkways, came to draw and preserve them. La Galerie Bretonne, produced by Oliver Perrin in 1838 and the second issue in 1856 under the title, Briez-Izel, ou la Vie des Bretons dans L'Armorique, provided the inspiration for many of Alfred Beau's enormously successful *scenes bretonnes.* The Galerie Armoricaine produced by Hippolyte Lalaisse in 1846 provided hundreds of studies, showing costumes, *coiffes* and figures in working poses; these were lavishly reproduced on faience by the Henriot firm in the early twentieth century. Both of these collections celebrated the color and charm of Breton customs. They showed details of the life and worship, the farmhouse interiors, the stone calvaries of the faithful, market scenes, costumes, etc. found all over Brittany. These watercolors fostered a pride and interest in the local scene which when translated to the local pottery gave Quimper ware new excitement and impetus. Though the argument has never been settled as to which factory, HB or Porquier, first started painting the little figure, *le petit breton* on the pottery, it became a symbol so attractive that it has inspired copies and counterfeits from all over the world during the last, almost one hundred years.

46. Quimper Plate 9½" diameter. Decoration: *demi-fantaisie.* Henriot factory, 1940s. (Private Collection)

47. Watercolor from Galerie Armoricaine by F. Hippolyte Lalaisse, 1845. Inspiration for Henriot decoration on plate #46.

48. Quimper Platter 17" x 11". Scene of a mother and children waving to the train. *Décor riche* border with Breton shield. Marked: HB Quimper. First Quarter of the 20th cent. (Private Collection)

The *petit breton* pattern continues to be a best seller for Quimper; however, the factories have had the good sense to keep innovating. Art déco pieces, the ODETTA line of artistic *grès* ware, the embroidery patterns are examples of this innovative spirit; also apple designs, the *Pecheur* series showing fishermen and their sweethearts, peasant figures from other regions — Provence, Les Landes, Pyrénées, Auvergne. By adjusting and adapting, Quimper has always maintained a fresh approach and a young attitude. Though the mixing and firing of the clay, the blending of the colors and glazes has been mechanized and modern kilns have been installed, the painting and decoration are still all done by hand. This is rare in an industry where stencils, decals and other prefabricated designs have generally been adopted.

The new management is determined to retain the factory in Quimper and to preserve the tradition of hand painting. Furthermore, it seeks to attract and reward with prizes or stipends those young and aspiring artists whose work will continue to enliven the Quimper product.

50. Quimper Cup and saucer ***Mouchoir*** pattern by POL, Henriot factory, 1930s. (Private Collection)

51. Quimper Plate 11" diameter, *Broderie* decoration made by applying colored glazes over cobalt glaze foundation, as one would decorate a cake *(à la poire)*. HB factory, 1940. (Private Collection)

49. Quimper 3 Groups of Figures 4" tall. Part of a set of eight couples at an Auvergne wedding, by André Galland. Series G. Henriot factory, 1930. (Private Collection)

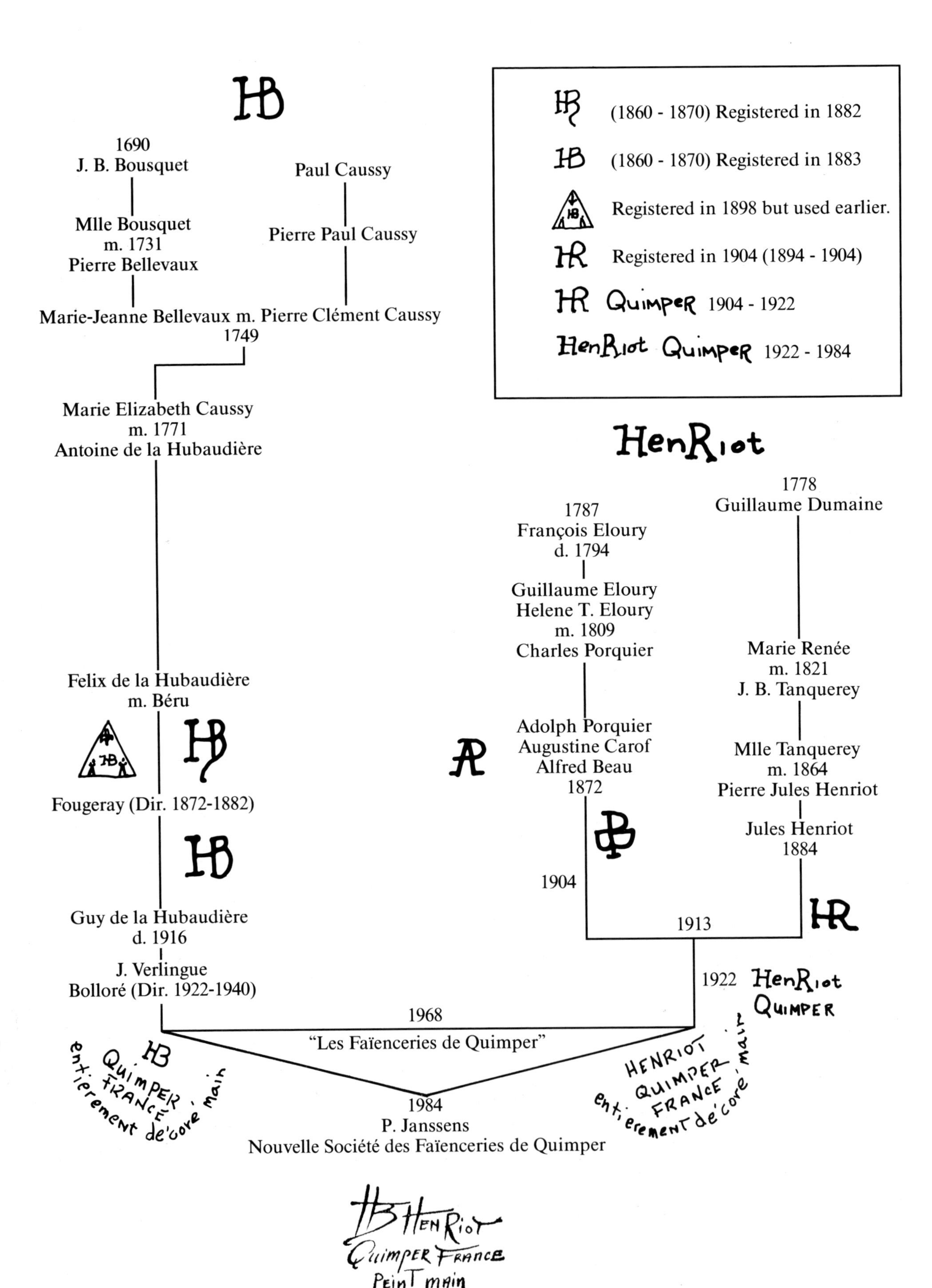
HB
1690
J. B. Bousquet
Mlle Bousquet
m. 1731
Pierre Bellevaux
Paul Caussy
Pierre Paul Caussy
Marie-Jeanne Bellevaux m. Pierre Clément Caussy
1749
Marie Elizabeth Caussy
m. 1771
Antoine de la Hubaudière
Felix de la Hubaudière
m. Béru
Fougeray (Dir. 1872-1882)
Guy de la Hubaudière
d. 1916
J. Verlingue
Bolloré (Dir. 1922-1940)
(1860 - 1870) Registered in 1882
(1860 - 1870) Registered in 1883
Registered in 1898 but used earlier.
Registered in 1904 (1894 - 1904)
HR Quimper 1904 - 1922
HenRiot Quimper 1922 - 1984
HenRiot
1787
François Eloury
d. 1794
Guillaume Eloury
Helene T. Eloury
m. 1809
Charles Porquier
Adolph Porquier
Augustine Carof
Alfred Beau
1872
1904
1778
Guillaume Dumaine
Marie Renée
m. 1821
J. B. Tanquerey
Mlle Tanquerey
m. 1864
Pierre Jules Henriot
Jules Henriot
1884
HR
1913
1922 HenRiot Quimper
1968
"Les Faïenceries de Quimper"
HB Quimper France entièrement décoré main
HENRIOT QUIMPER FRANCE entièrement décoré main
1984
P. Janssens
Nouvelle Société des Faïenceries de Quimper
HB HenRiot Quimper France Peint main

Boulogne-sur-Mer

In 1773 Louis-Marie Verlingue founded a faiencerie, assisted by Jean de Villeneuve, a chemist from La Rochelle. His products were composed of a fine quality clay, which made a light *pâte;* this was covered with a good glaze. His decorations were mostly in the genre of Rouen, but he used a characteristic color yellow, known as "yellow of Naples" — clear and lemony. Verlingue also made ordinary pottery and tiles with blue decoration outlined in brown.

As a result of the 1786 treaty, Verlingue closed shop and went to Amiens. In 1798, he moved to Desvres. We do not hear any more of his work.

For several generations the Verlingue family did not work in faience. Then, in 1903, Jules Verlingue, a young descendent, established a new faiencerie at 183, rue de Brequerecque in Boulogne. He made *fantaisie* pieces very much like the souvenir and *fantaisie* items currently being made at Desvres. Verlingue's mark was: VJT.

52. Boulogne-sur-Mer Ermine figurine 4" long. Emblem of Anne de Bretagne. Verlingue factory, Early 20th cent. (Private Collection)

Early in his career, Jules Verlingue benefited from the advice and support of a M. Louis. Some of the faience products made at this time were marked to include Louis' name in the signature. The mark was: L↓V

53. Boulogne-sur-Mer Menu card 5" high, marked: Paimpol. Verlingue factory, Early 20th cent. (Private Collection)

In 1917, Jules Verlingue bought the de la Hubaudière (HB) factory in Quimper and moved his family to that city. Around 1920, he sold his firm in Boulogne to Henri Delcourt who continued producing the same kinds of wares Verlingue had made popular.

Henri Delcourt took the mark H↓D for his factory's productions.

54. Boulogne-sur-Mer Donkey double salt figure 4" x 3¾". On his saddle: *"Bien faire et laisser braire"*. Roughly translated "Do it right and let him bray (complain)". Made for Mont Fort l'Amaury by Delcourt factory, 1930s. (Private Collection)

The author wishes to thank Mme. Jules Verlingue for providing this information.

Desvres

The town of Desvres is situated eighteen kilometers from Boulogne in the department of Pas de Calais. From earliest times it has been an important center for pottery. During excavations at Belle Croix in 1950, a Gallo-Roman kiln was unearthed containing several objects ready for firing.

Various texts in the 13th and 14th centuries refer to the potters of Desvres. Rue de Potiers gives evidence also to a long association of potters with the town.

In the 18th century, neighboring potting centers such as Hesdin, Aire, Boulogne, St. Omer, Lille, St. Amand, Calais, Bailleul and Vron were well-known. Potters traveled from center to center, also to Desvres, reproducing faience which borrowed heavily from the great Delft tradition. Known as *faïences du Nord,* these factories are often overlooked when compared to the *Cinq Grands* of the 18th century: Marseilles, Moustiers, Nevers, Rouen, and Strasbourg.

Caught in the social, political and economic struggles between Flanders, France and England, these faienceries did not fare well toward the end of the 18th century. Most of them succumbed in the period of Napoleon's wars and their records are lost. Few of the pieces that survived are marked, so it is difficult, sometimes impossible, to distinguish the products of each faiencerie. Most of the examples show the same kinds of designs: simple flowers, a rose in manganese, heavy strokes, naive and rustic in execution.

55. **Desvres** Table and chair trinket containers with lids. Géo Martel factory for Châtelguyon. Early 20th cent. (Private Collection)

The later Desvres productions, those of the mid-19th and early 20th centuries, reflect a unique decorative combination of the northern tradition — Delft, and the western tradition — Rouen. Added to which, we find a touch of whimsy in the animal shapes, the bric-a-brac items which developed at the end of the 19th century in response to the desire for such trinkets on the part of the emerging merchant class, the new tourist and the more affluent bourgeoisie. This new market supported the production of several faienceries in Desvres, particularly those of the Fourmaintraux family.

56. **Desvres** Menu card 5¼" x 3¼" Breton crest, Rouen type tassle border. Florals on reverse. Marked: 589 Mont St. Michel. Early 20th cent. (Private Collection)

The patriarch of the family, François-Joseph Fourmaintraux (in the early records spelled Fourmentraux) was born in Lille in 1764. He came to Desvres in 1791, married Mlle Benard in 1797 and worked as a painter/turner in the STA faiencerie. He opened his own establishment in 1804, the beginning of a long line of Fourmaintraux potters. Three sons followed in the tradition: Louis-François, Alexandre-Joseph and Antoine.

The two youngest, Alexandre-Joseph and Antoine took over their father's factory in 1841, when he died. They continued the production of tiles and common dishware until 1866, when Antoine died. At that time,

Alexandre sold his portion of the business to his eldest brother, Louis-François. This brother had left Desvres in 1835 and traveled to Beauvais, Forges-les-Eaux, and Paris (rue de la Roquette) where he worked as a turner and painter. Around 1841, he returned to Desvres and opened his own factory at the end of the rue de Potiers, in the area known as "Le Gazon". Here he made square tiles and *objects de fantaisie.* His factory was known for the production of *jacquelines,* pitchers in the shape of a seated grandmother or grandfather; also pipes made in the form of Turk's heads, as well as other amusing bric-a-brac.

When Louis-François died in 1885, he left six sons, three of whom continued in the potting trade. The oldest, François, married Mlle Courquin in 1862 and started his own establishment at Belle Croix in 1863. Here new techniques were introduced; new presses for making tiles replaced the old method of forming the squares by hand. Around 1872, the factory began producing specialty items for the retail trade. Aided by his wife, who took charge of the decoration, Fourmaintraux-Courquin began making cachepots, jardinières, plates, platters, candlesticks, etc. based on the designs and décors of the old faiences of Rouen, Delft, Nevers, and Moustiers. These pieces are marked with an interlaced F.C. thus:

Two other brothers, Jules, born in 1845 and Emile, born in 1857, maintained their father's business at Le Gazon. They worked together from 1877 to 1887, specializing in the reproduction of the old faiences. The mark of this association is two Fs with a number below; thus:

57. **Desvres** Tea tile 6" square. Rouen decoration: basket of flowers, lambrequin border. Marked: ROUEN in blue. Early 20th cent. (Private Collection)

58. **Desvres** Hanging match holder 5" x 3" Breton crest with Rouen type floral decoration. Fourmaintraux-Courquin factory, Late 19th cent. (Private Collection)

59. Desvres Vase, five openings, 4" tall. Rouen type *á la corne* decoration with florals and red chain border. Probably Fourmaintraux-Courquin, Late 19th cent.

60. Desvres Pair of candlesticks 8½" tall. Rouen type decoration. Fourmaintraux Frères factory, Late 19th cent.

61. Desvres Wall sconce 5" tall. Rouen *à la corne* decoration with red chain border. Fourmaintraux Frères factory, Late 19th cent.

From 1877 on, experiments were made to improve the quality of the clay, glaze and decoration applied to the copies of the old faience in order to make them more authentic. With the help of his wife, Elisa Moison, Emile made objects particularly in the Rouen style with décors *à la corne, au panier fleuri* (the flower basket), *aux lambrequins, aux coquilles, au style rocaille,* with flowers, birds, and insects, edges and border designs which resembled more and more the glaze and vivid colors of Rouen.

Emile traveled to Normandy and Brittany in search of ideas and to determine the market for various designs. Here he came across the popular Breton figures of Quimper and the interest in traditional costumes which was so prevalent in Normandy and Brittany at that time. These ideas were incorporated in the production of the Fourmaintraux Frères.

In 1887 Emile withdrew from the joint association and Jules continued the paternal enterprise at Le Gazon, making tiles and ordinary dishware. Later he too began to make artistic imitations of Rouen, Nevers, Marseilles, Moustiers, Strasbourg and Delft faiences. This establishment was sold to François Masse in 1903. The name changed to Masse Frères under the direction of

Jacques Masse and his brother, Robert, in 1948.

In 1980 M.J. Muselet took over the enterprise, which is now known as *Masse "Artisans Faïenciers".* They continue to make copies of the old faiences for which they have six thousand different molds. In 1966 they were awarded the *Prestige de France* commendation.

In 1899, Emile Fourmaintraux began a new factory at La Poterie, with the assistance of his son, Gabriel, who had attended art school at Sèvres. From 1902 to 1934, this factory produced a rare collection of *objets d'art* in fine porcelain: decorative plates, lamps, miniatures, candy dishes, etc. which were world re-knowned. Then, as a result of the 1925 exposition, interest returned to faience in the old tradition and the factory reverted to making those kinds of items: wall pockets, religious statues, oyster plates, etc. in the *grand feu* method.

63. Desvres Plate 9¾" diameter. Song: *"Yann Guenille".* Marked: ROUEN 1708 in blue. ROUEN indicates the design; the number is a factory code, not a date. Early 20th cent.

62. Desvres Horse statue 4½" tall. Miniature copy of 17th century Delft original. Masse factory, 1984. (Private Collection)

64. Desvres Plate 9¾" diameter. Song : *"Le Clocher à Jour" St. Pol de Léon,* based on Rouen Aria plates. Fourmaintraux-Courquin factory. Late 19th cent.

65. **Desvres** Car 4½" long. Possibly used as a candy dish or a double salt server. Rouen crest, Rouen border designs. Marked: ROUEN in blue. Early 20th cent. (Private Collection)

Under the direction of Gabriel Fourmaintraux in the 1930s (his mark was) then assisted by his son, Claude and his son-in-law, Daniel Dutertre, the faiencerie at La Poterie evolved into the present firm: *"G. & C. Fourmaintraux et Dutertre"* which today makes ancient reproductions, publicity articles, bathroom fixtures, lamps, all sorts of decorative and useful objects in faience.

The original Fourmaintraux-Courquin factory which became *"Charles Fourmaintraux,"* then in 1946, *"S.A. Fourmaintraux-Delassus",* merged in 1984 with another society, *M.C.M. (Mosaique Ceramique de Montplaisir).* Together they produce wall and floor coverings and the adhesive products to attach them. Their mark is **DESVRES.**

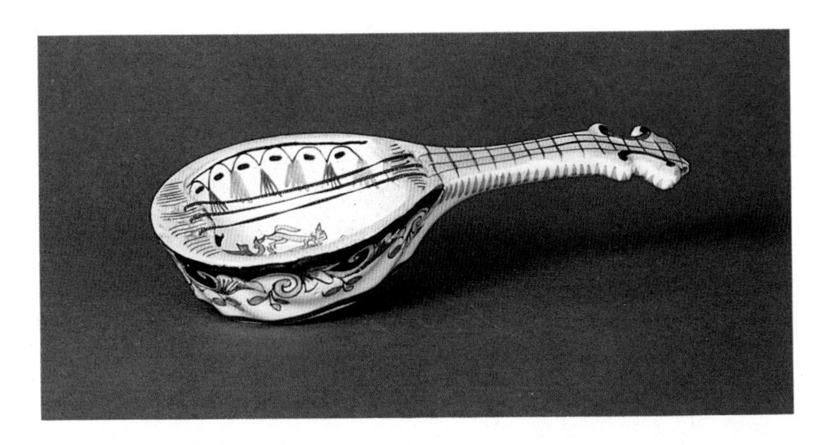

66. **Desvres** Mandolin ashtray 7" long. Breton crest decoration in bowl. Rouen border design. Marked: MG Dinard. Geó Martel factory, 1920s.

Two other factories at Desvres which were formed outside of the Fourmaintraux family bear attention. The first had its beginnings around 1806, under the direction of Jean-François-César Boulongue. This factory passed through two more generations until 1848 when the only grandson, Antoine-César, died. The factory was sold to Louis-François Level in 1850 and transmitted in 1888, at his death, to the youngest son, Gaeton Level.

Gaeton followed the tradition established at the other faienceries in Desvres at the time and produced copies of the old classics. In 1900, the factory was acquired by Géo Martel, who moved the site from the Pont d'Echau to the area of Longfosse, near the Chausée Brunehaut, where it is today.

In 1954, under Jacques Martel's direction, the factory experienced some reverses and closed temporarily. In 1957 - 1958 it opened again as *"La Société Géo Martel"* under the direction of Jacques Tallier. In 1964, Jacques Guillerme became the director of the company which is now called *"La Société Nouvelle des Etablissements Géo Martel". "Géo Martel"* continues to produce copies of old faience: Moustiers, Rouen, Strasbourg, Nevers, Marseilles, etc. Their mark is: MG

The second factory which was independent of the Fourmaintraux tradition was founded in 1947 by René Delarue. His production inclines more to the artistic rather than the copyist. A small concern, they make original forms by hand, in the old tradition of *grand feu,* though with a futuristic look.

67. **Desvres** Mustard pot 3" x 4½" in the shape of two pigs at a trough. Spoon forms curled tail of the larger pig. Geó Martel factory, 1984. (Private Collection)

Desvres has more than any other center kept alive the interest, the variety and the spirit of Rouen, particularly through the repeated use of the traditional decorations. Most of the older (fifty to a hundred years) examples marked ROUEN which collectors admire today are not 18th century Rouen items, but more often are late 19th and early 20th century Desvres creations. The colors are rich; the designs are attractive, full of hand-painted detail and the molds are endearing. *Objets de fantaisie,* amusing animals, whimsical containers for cigars, mustard, trinkets, etc. are only part of the vast repertoire of these factories.

Today these firms: Fourmaintraux-Dutertre, Géo Martel, and Masse still produce copies of the old faience and souvenir items to appeal to the modest collector and the tourist. These items can be found in the gift shops and souvenir stands all over France.

Fourmentraux

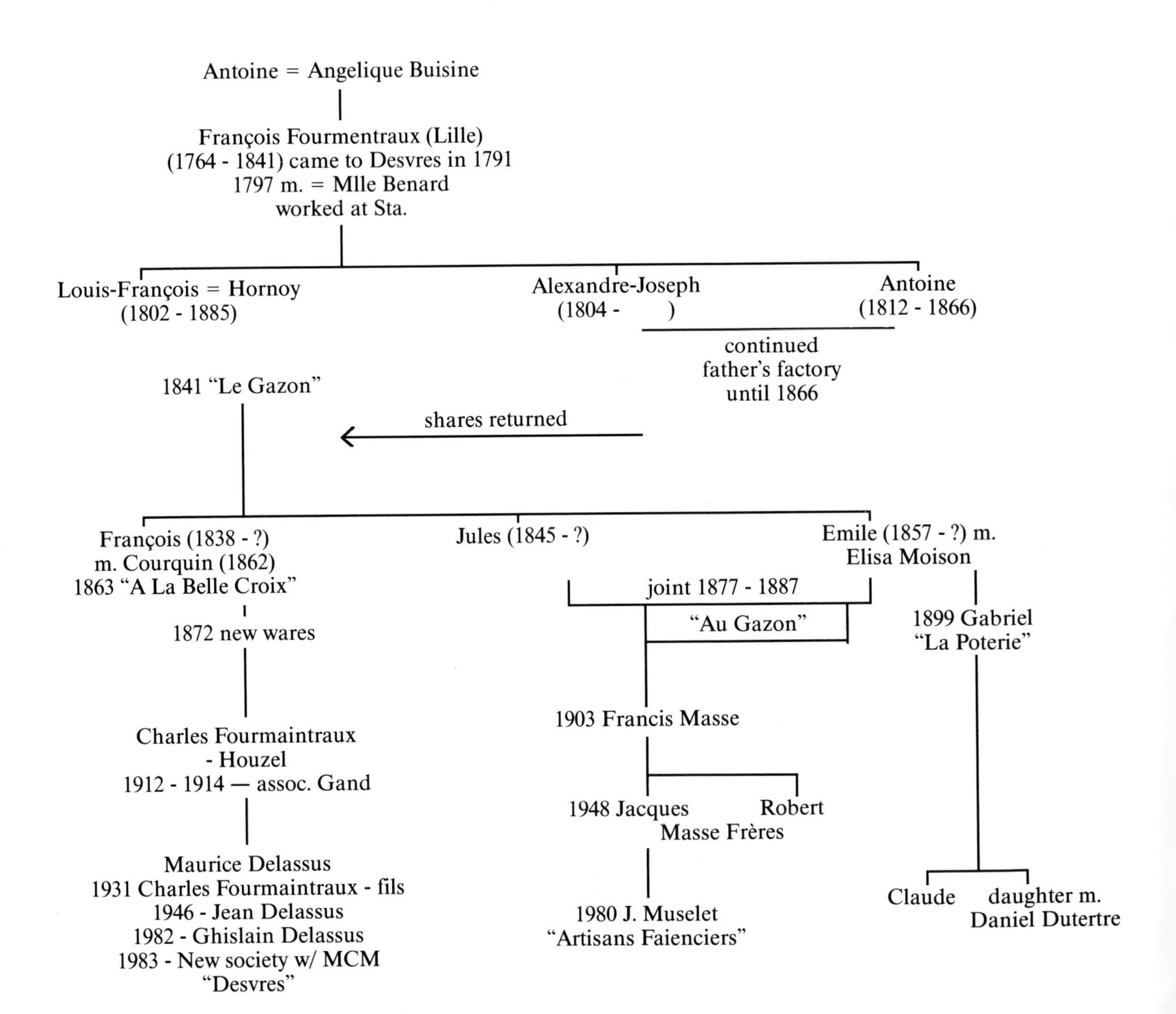

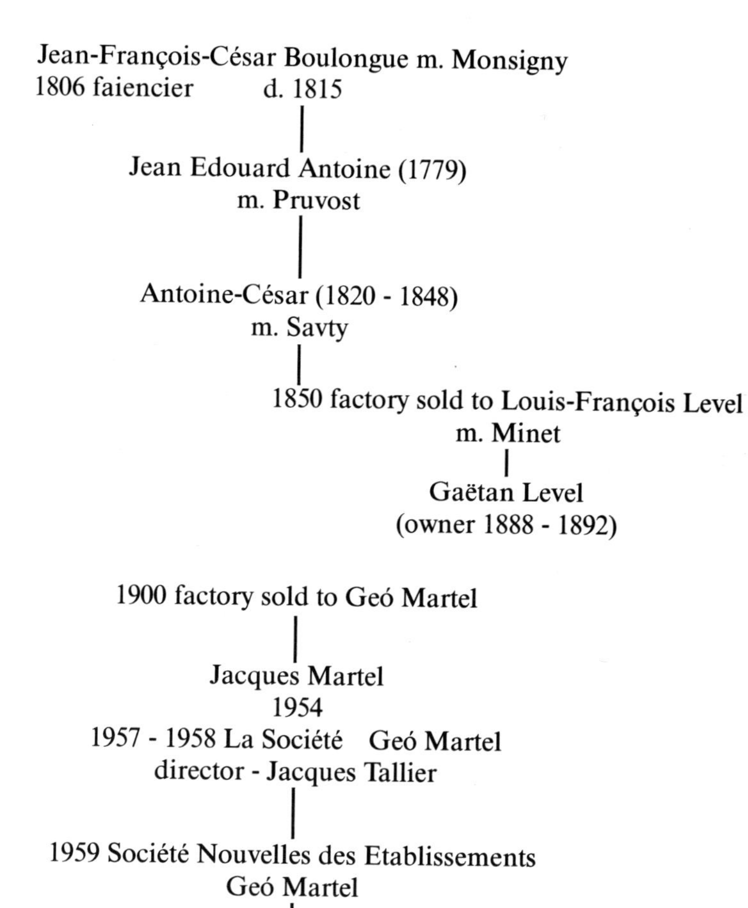
Jean-François-César Boulongue m. Monsigny
1806 faiencier d. 1815
Jean Edouard Antoine (1779)
m. Pruvost
Antoine-César (1820 - 1848)
m. Savty
1850 factory sold to Louis-François Level
m. Minet
Gaëtan Level
(owner 1888 - 1892)
1900 factory sold to Geó Martel
Jacques Martel
1954
1957 - 1958 La Société Geó Martel
director - Jacques Tallier
1959 Société Nouvelles des Etablissements
Geó Martel
1964 M. Jacques Guillerme

68. Malicorne Platter 22" x 9½". Market scene taken from Quimper original. Marked: St. Malo, Late 19th cent. (Private Collection)

69. Malicorne Serving bowl 10½" diameter, excluding handles. Green *décor riche* border, shield and ermine tail design copies Porquier of Quimper. Marked: PBx, Late 19th cent. (Private Collection)

Malicorne

Malicorne is in the Sarthe region of France, in the ancient province of Maine, between Le Mans and La Flèche. Originally called Condate from Condé, meaning confluent, the town is situated at the junction of the Sarthe and the Vezanne rivers. At the end of the 12th century, the town changed its name to Malicorne, which means "bad horn". This name referred to the sharp point of land which, though it enclosed an ancient fortress, jutted into the river making defense difficult and navigation treacherous.

Because of the richness of the local clays and the abundance of firewood in the area, groups of potters had been active in this region since the Gallo-Roman era. Probably the most important ceramic produced in this district was the glazed pottery of Ligron, which reached its zenith in the 15th and 16th centuries. This was not a true faience, but a *poterie vernisée,* made by using different types and colors of clay in contrast and glazed, but not painted. The characteristic color of the ware is yellowish, speckled and dribbled with green, blue or manganese. The tone is grayish and the glaze is never even or clear.

The Ligron potters produced many decorations: animals, flowers, etc., but they are best known for creating many statues of the Virgin. The oldest of these figurines is a statue of the nursing Virgin, the production of which was prohibited after the Council of Trent in 1563.

Ligron pottery, though highly esteemed in the region never adapted to the manufacture of faience which became most popular in the 18th century. All vestiges of the technique finished in 1905 when the last potter closed down his kiln.

In 1747, Jean Loiseau, a native of the Touraine, set up a faiencerie in Malicorne, drawn by the proximity of raw materials and markets in Le Mans, Angers, La Flèche and Nantes. He hired turners and painters from Ligron and Nevers, where he had worked previously. Understandably, the production of Loiseau's faiencerie echoed the Nevers style: designs incorporating a sprinkling of blue flowers *(semis de fleurs bleus)* outlined in manganese and later, polychromed flowers and ornamentation.

In 1785, Jean Louis succeeded his father and brought in workers from other regions whose experience enlarged the repertoire of the factory. The production at Malicorne throughout the 18th century copied all known styles. For everyday use they produced barber bowls, vases, pitchers, jugs, tobacco jars etc. For decorative uses they made special items including holy water fonts, Virgin statues, crucifixes and plaques. These were made in the styles of Nevers, Moustiers, Rouen and Strasbourg.

During the last part of the 18th century, the faience business suffered throughout France. We have seen how the preference for porcelain and the competition with cheaper English imports drove many faienceries out of business. Under Napoleon's régime, particularly his Continental Blockade, local industries revived somewhat, but not consistently. The big centers at Rouen went into serious and fatal decline, while other potting centers expanded. Smaller factories had a higher success rate, especially if they could depend on the support of their local customers.

In 1829 Jean-Louis Loiseau sold the faiencerie to Charles Cador, who formed an association with Loiseau's son-in-law, Jules Béatrix. The name of the factory became Cador-Béatrix and passed in time to Jules II Béatrix, the son. Other faienceries which were founded in the

Malicorne area in the early 19th century were: Meneville, Prieuré, Sablon, and Bourg Joly.

By 1850 Malicorne products were indistinguishable from any of the other copies of the great centers. It was not until Léon Pouplard arrived on the scene that Malicorne developed its own style.

Léon Pouplard was born in Angers in 1865. In 1888 he married Marie-Angèle Béatrix, daughter of Jules II Béatrix and the former Mlle Pellerin. Pouplard became apprentice in the faiencerie of his wife's widowed grandmother, Mme. Veuve Jules I Béatrix. He took over the factory in 1890, at her death.

70. Malicorne Double corne wall pocket 7" tall. Breton figures and blue two-toned fleur-de-lys. Marked: ¶B, Late 19th cent.

71. Malicorne Barber bowl 10½" x 8". Design shows direct imitation of Quimper figures. No mark. Late 19th cent. (Private Collection)

In 1891, as a result of his travels and researches Pouplard brought back from Brittany ideas and designs using the Breton figure, modeled after the drawings by Lalaisse and the decorations of Alfred Beau at Quimper. He used the Breton motif on plates, bowls, wallpockets, crucifixes, statues (particularly of the Virgin) and small souvenir items. These sold extremely well at the ocean and channel resort areas. In 1895 Pouplard hit upon a gimmick which would enhance his sales. He devised a signature for his wares which would combine his initial P

72. Malicorne Plate 9½" Breton scene with woman and child at roadside shrine *(calvaire)*. Border and shield copied from Porquier's copyrighted design; signature on reverse has been scratched off, Late 19th cent. (Private Collection)

with that of his wife, B (for Béatrix). The early version was qB which later became PBx . Harmless enough at first glance, this signature had been purposely designed to confuse the buyer into thinking he was purchasing a Quimper product of the Porquier factory, whose great artist was Alfred Beau. There the desired signature was a P with a B on its side, thus: ꟼB

As a result of this chicanerie, a lawsuit ensued in 1897 which Pouplard lost. His faiencerie was obliged to discard/destroy all stock marked with his P.B. signature. In theory, all pieces bearing the PBx signature with Breton figures, copied from the Quimper designs must date from 1891 to 1898. We have seen plates from this period on which the mark has been gouged off, presumably to comply with the terms of the law suit. Whether the legal decision required Pouplard to destroy his pieces with designs from other regions, e.g. Normandy, we have no solid information. We have seen a cup and saucer with a World War I decoration, marked: 1914 - 1918 and PBx . Therefore, the piece had to date from 1918 or later. As far as we know, Pouplard continued to use the PBx signature on the non-Breton designed products of his faiencerie up to its closing in 1952.

73. Water color from <u>Galerie Armoricaine</u> by F. Hippolyte Lalaisse, 1845. Shows man in costume of Carhaix.

74. Malicorne Plate 9½" diameter. Breton figure based on Lalaisse's drawing #73. Border and shield taken from Porquier in Quimper. Mark on back has been scratched off. Late 19th cent. (Private Collection)

From his school days, Pouplard was a naturalist. He had a fine collection of stuffed birds which he produced in ceramic in the style of Copenhagen. During the 1920s the Malicorne factory also produced fish and mammal figures.

After the First World War, Pouplard's reputation grew. He sent examples of his work to the finest shops in Paris. His art was featured in the *ateliers* of *Primavera,* the special design shop of *Le Printemps.*

Pouplard's wife died in 1923, but he continued to produce his wares according to the old methods up to 1952. He mixed three earths, the gray clay of Malicorne with the red and gray earths of La Suze. The glazes also were prepared at the faiencerie. The ovens, fired only once every two weeks, were heated by wood dried for three years. In an open, three tiered, beehive shaped kiln, three types of pottery were baked at one time; the brown ware which baked at the highest temperature was placed at the bottom; the decorated faience stood in the center and at the top, the biscuit pieces.

Pouplard died in 1954, without heirs.

In 1898 or 1899, a young painter-decorator came to work for Pouplard. His name was Emile Tessier. Son of a ceramist, Emile had always worked in clay. He apprenticed himself at various factories in the area, learning techniques and designs from them all. In 1924, he started his own factory with his brother-in-law, Laze. They separated two years later.

Tessier had two daughters. One married Valentin Villarmé, an artist and decorator at the factory who later became professor of ceramics at the Beaux Arts school in Le Mans. The other daughter, Odette, married Roger Després in 1929. On the occasion of her marriage, Mme. Després received a present from her father's

75. Malicorne Creel bank 3½" x 3". Decoration is copied from Quimper Breton figure. Pouplard factory. Late 19th cent. (Private Collection)

76. Malicorne Photograph of Pouplard in his studio, 1940s.

confrères in the faience business — it was a large Quimper vase from the **ODETTA** collection, chosen because of the similarity of the names. Their son carried on the production of the *"Faïenceries Tessier"* until 1984 when it was sold to Victor Deschang, a business man from Metz.

Tessier's great contribution to Malicorne faience was the rediscovery of the Ligron open work pottery. Using a more resilient clay from the Meudon region and installing the first muffle kiln in Malicorne to produce faience by the *petit feu* method, Tessier started to produce elegant baskets with delicately cut out lattice work, often embellished with flowers and fruits.

Before 1940, the Tessier factory was the most important in the area. Ninety-nine workers produced thousands of artistic pieces in the style of Delft, Nevers, Moustiers, Rouen and Strasbourg. But hard times came to the faienceries at Malicorne as they have to most of the other potting centers of France.

Currently, under M. Deschang's direction, the faiencerie employs twelve workers. They export to the Mediterranean Shop in New York. The factory's name is *"Faïenceries d'art de Malicorne"*. The mark of the production continues to be the same as it was under Tessier.

77. Malicorne Old post card of the Pouplard-Béatrix faiencerie, showing Emile Tessier on the left and Marius Moreau on the right.

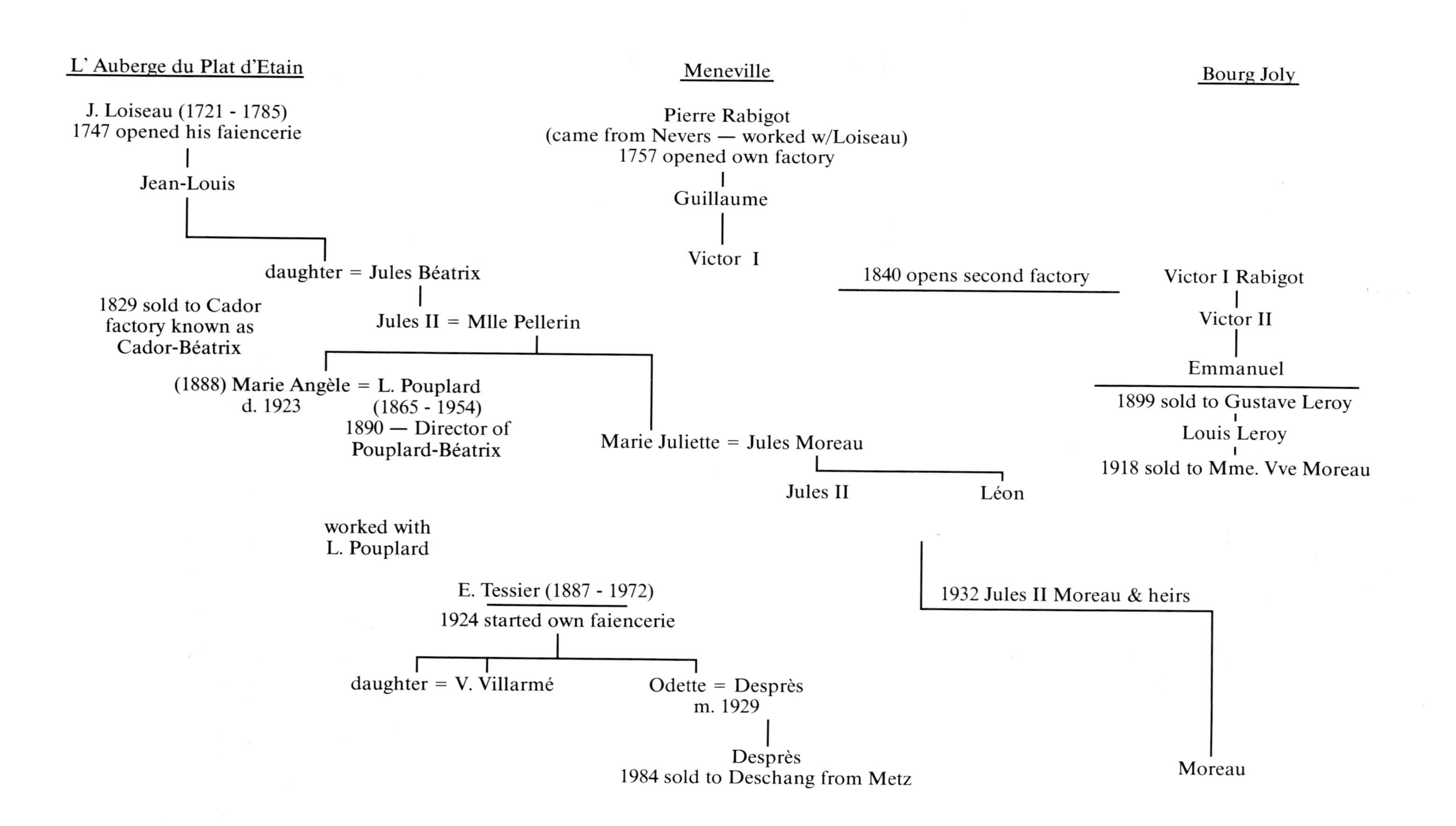
L' Auberge du Plat d'Etain
J. Loiseau (1721 - 1785)
1747 opened his faiencerie
Jean-Louis
daughter = Jules Béatrix
1829 sold to Cador
factory known as
Cador-Béatrix
Jules II = Mlle Pellerin
(1888) Marie Angèle = L. Pouplard
d. 1923
(1865 - 1954)
1890 — Director of
Pouplard-Béatrix
Marie Juliette = Jules Moreau
Jules II
Léon
worked with
L. Pouplard
E. Tessier (1887 - 1972)
1924 started own faiencerie
daughter = V. Villarmé
Odette = Desprès
m. 1929
Desprès
1984 sold to Deschang from Metz
Meneville
Pierre Rabigot
(came from Nevers — worked w/Loiseau)
1757 opened own factory
Guillaume
Victor I
1840 opens second factory
Bourg Joly
Victor I Rabigot
Victor II
Emmanuel
1899 sold to Gustave Leroy
Louis Leroy
1918 sold to Mme. Vve Moreau
1932 Jules II Moreau & heirs
Moreau

78. Blois Old post card of Ulysse faiencerie, showing the modelers' studio.

79. Blois Old post card of Ulysse faiencerie, showing a kiln in the factory.

Blois

Jean Judes Ulysse Besnard was born in Blois in 1826. He studied in Paris to be an easel painter; returned to Blois in 1858, where he put on several exhibits of his paintings. His topics which were often historical, showed a decidedly Italian flavor. He specialized in recreating the personalities and the events of the château at Blois and for these representations he won several awards. Around 1861, he shortened his name to Ulysse, which became his artistic signature. From that time until 1884, Ulysse divided his time among several occupations; being a painter, a restorer of art works and being the first curator of the Blois museum which is housed in the château.

Early in 1862, Ulysse began to experiment with producing decorated faience. At first he worked with a fellow faiencier, Monsnergue, using Monsnergue's clay and kiln. But soon he started mixing his own clays and glazes and constructed his own muffle kiln. As a painter not familiar with the potter's trade, Ulysse taught himself all the steps and techniques of faience making, sustaining many failures on the way. But, by the end of that year, he was sufficiently assured of his success that he founded his own faiencerie on the Quai des Iberts at the Croix des Pelerins. This was the site of an ancient hostel-convent where the pilgrims stopped on their way to the shrine of St. Jacques de Compostello. The shell, a symbol of St. James, and the cross became Ulysse's mark. The V in the center is his initial, a U written in the roman style.

80. Blois Covered jar 2½" diameter. Rope and tassel emblem of Anne de Bretagne decorates the lid. Balon factory, August 1909. (Private Collection)

Ulysse was an artist and an experimenter. While he continued to paint on canvas, he became more intrigued with the challenge of faience making. This was the period (1850 - 1870) when the knowledge of science

81. Blois Wallpocket 3½" x 4" Salamander emblem of François I. Balon factory. No date. (Private Collection)

82. Blois Wallpocket 3½" x 4" Pierced swan emblem of Claude de France and Louise de Savoie. Balon factory, October 1907. (Private Collection)

and technology advanced rapidly and was frequently reported in the current journals. These articles stimulated activity in many areas, but particularly they revived interest in the old faiences. It was thought that the new technology could recapture the process of making Italian and Hispano-Moresque majolica and that new methods could duplicate the famous French faiences of the 17th and 18th centuries.

Ulysse studied carefully; he made elegant and meticulous drawings for his work. His decorations and molds were extremely delicate and refined. The influence of Italian majolica is very evident on the urns and ewers he produced. The forms and the décors of the Renaissance are seen in the tendrils, the masks, lion heads, sirens and chimera which are featured in the decoration and on the handles of his pieces.

Ulysses's factory produced both little trinkets and large decorative works. It is thought that he produced the smaller wares as a way to experiment with new designs, to attract clients and to earn some money. As he gained success, he made fewer of the small pieces and launched into making larger examples of artistic importance.

In 1865, he employed five workers: one molder, Henri Allaire; the rest were decorators: J. Tortat, Ernest Rouveyre, Eugene Verra, and Adrien Thibault. According to the personal records of these workers, Ulysse ran his factory like a family and he was the Papa. He taught all the artists his skills and encouraged each to develop his own specialty. Working in a family setting, one of the employees would read aloud to the others as they worked.

During the first ten years (1862 - 1872) Ulysse experimented with several styles. His Rouen expressions were characterized by a yellow background and black tracery, the *niellé* pattern; or by the lambrequins and flower basket designs of early Rouen. As his style developed, he moved toward painting entire scenes on faience. He specialized in depicting 16th century kings and queens in historic situations, often centering on events which took place at the château in Blois.

In his position as curator of the château, Ulysse took great pride in publicising the magnificent buildings. Recently the Commission of Historic Monuments had restored the François I and the Louis XII wings which had been badly damaged during the Revolution. The stone engravings which pictured the royal emblems over the doorways and fireplaces had been scratched off by the "patriots" and only after long and arduous reconstruction had these sculptures been made visible again. Ulysse celebrated these emblems in his faience. His most popular decorations became the initials and mottos of the French kings and queens who had lived at Blois. On his smaller wares — the ashtrays, candy dishes, pin trays and wall pockets appear the *porc-épic* of Louis XII, the salamander of François I, the ermine of Anne de Bretagne, and the pierced swan of Claude and/or Louise de Savoie.

83. **Blois** Pot 2¼" high. Italian Renaissance style decoration. Balon factory, September 1908. (Private Collection)

From 1868, to 1884, the Ulysse factory was at its height; 23,000 pieces were produced during this period — pieces of great quality in all ranges from the large decorative platters, vases and urns to the small inkwells, cups and small trays. His mark, the shell and cross with the inscription *"Ulysse à Blois"* appeared on almost all his work. Several variations included the shell with *Ulysse* only, or the shell with *Blois* or simply B written in script underneath.

In 1886 Ulysse left Blois and retired to his property in Brittany. He leased his house to Emile Balon and his wife, and in 1887, he sold to the same Emile Balon, his business, clients, materiel and the new merchandise. Ulysse remained associated with the firm until 1891;

during this time the factory mark remained as before.

Around 1891 Ulysse seems to have ceased contributing to the production. At that point, Balon adapted the shell and cross mark to include *"Ulysse à Blois, E. Balon Succ."*, signifying Balon as Ulysse's successor.

Ulysse died in 1899.

84. Blois Old post card of Ulysse faiencerie showing the painting workshop.

Emile Balon (1859 - 1929) had been first an apprentice and later a decorator with Ulysse. In 1886 he took over the direction of the factory while Ulysse was in semiretirement. Balon was not the artist innovator that Ulysse was; instead he was more of a technician and a merchant. The lease agreement that he had with Ulysse's daughter cost him very dearly, so he sought new markets for his goods to pay the heavy debts. He continued the production of trinkets and souvenirs with the royal emblems which he sent to the beach resorts and to the watering places, to shops and tourist centers all over France, Monaco, Belgium, Holland and Germany. He put together a publicity package of samples, postcards, and photographs of his factory to advertise his wares.

Where Ulysse had entered the great expositions with important creations and won prizes in artistic competitions, Balon found it more economical for him to produce small items for sale to the public. In the years 1910 to 1914, he exhibited in the small home shows. His work was considered moderately priced and appealed to the middle class clients who bought these items as wedding, confirmation and birthday presents, or as souvenirs of a trip to the Loire valley. Records show that Balon's faience was shipped to England, New York, Boston, etc.

In 1914, Balon left the original Ulysse property and bought new quarters for himself and the factory. The war, unfortunately, interfered with the initial success of the new faiencerie and it had to close temporarily. After the war, production resumed. The number of employees grew from five workers in 1920 to seven workers in 1927. In that year Gaston Bruneau, Balon's son-in-law, added his signature to the factory mark. From 1927 - 1929, the shell and cross mark included *"E. Balon G. Bruneau - Balon"*.

Balon died in 1929. He was succeeded by Gaston Bruneau and his wife, Balon's daughter. Bruneau lacked the commercial skills and the merchant sense that guided Balon's success; Mme. Bruneau possessed more of that aptitude. Under her supervision, the shop in town and the factory sales prospered from 1930 up to the war in 1940. The factory's fortunes declined after 1950 when Mme. Bruneau died. All activity at the faiencerie ceased in 1953.

Marks of the Ulysse factory:

1861 - 1889 The shell and cross motif with V; also an indication of the month and year of production. The roman numerals over the shell indicate the month; the arabic numerals on either side of the shell indicate the year.

VI
7 4
Ulysse à Blois

Ulysse Blois
E Balon Seur

1890 - 1929 Balon's mark as successor to Ulysse. The numerals indicating month and year of production were gradually eliminated as they interfered with marketing.

Ulysse à Blois
G Bruneau Balon
Sre d'E. Balon

1930 Bruneau's mark included "Ulysse à Blois
G. Bruneau - Balon
Seur d' E. Balon"
This proved too involved to paint on small surfaces. The mark was changed to:

G. Bruneau-Balon-Blois

1861 - 1889 On the later pieces, the shell and cross were eliminated.

Two other faienciers from Blois who worked at one time for Ulysse are Josaphat Tortat (1843 - ?) and Adrien Thibault (1844 - 1918).

Very little is known of Tortat and his work; his production years are short — 1873 to 1881. His style, resembling that of Ulysse, used the same Italian Renaissance designs which incorporated tendrils, masks, dolphins and grotesques; however, the execution of the products lacked the polish of the master. His mark is:

7 4
J. Tortat
BLOIS

Adrien Thibault worked at the Ulysse factory from 1864 to 1867 when he left for military service in the Italian wars. In 1872, when he returned to France, he worked at the faiencerie at Gien where he was made one of the chief decorators. He left Gien two years later and returned to the suburbs of Blois - La Chausée Saint-Victor, where he opened his own studio in his house.

Thibault created his own clays and models. Though his designs resemble those of Ulysse, having the same affinity for the Italian Renaissance décors, the process differed from that of Ulysse. Thibault painted on the raw surface of the biscuit and then immersed his piece in the glaze before the final firing. This was a more difficult process; his kiln was also very small, so many failures occurred. Thibault was able to produce only a very limited supply of exquisite pieces.

In 1918 he died, in the midst of production. His daughter and his granddaughters have preserved the house and his studio as a museum. Everything is maintained exactly as it was at the time of his death — the pieces in the kiln, those ready for firing, the tools and the paint pots are exactly as they were when he died.

Thibault's marks are:

85. Angoulême Lion statue. Sazerac manufacture, 18th cent. (Courtesy ABC Décor)

Angoulême

Many small faienceries operated in and around Angoulême during the century preceding the period which concerns this study. None appears to have dominated the scene for long, but their names and marks do occasionally appear on pieces in today's marketplace. The following list of factory owners and their workers should help to fix the operation of these faienceries chronologically.

Les Sazerac

In 1731 Louis Sazerac and Jacques Crouzat formed an association to found a faiencerie "Les Faux Roches" at Saintes. This was dissolved two years later.

In 1748 Bernard Sazerac founded a factory at L'Houmeau with his brother. When Bernard died in 1774, his widow and their son, Louis, continued the production until 1795 when the faiencerie was sold to Jean-Baptiste Glaumont, son-in-law to Louis. The factory stayed in this family until 1842 when François-Léon Durandeau took over the direction. From 1866 to 1882 Thomas & Cie. guided the production; the Lassuze family took over in 1882. Their marks were:

In 1888 Pineau and Patros registered this mark:
The factory closed in 1895.

Fleurat & Jucaud

In 1790 Pierre Fleurat (called Pinguet) was a turner at the Sazerac factory. In 1791, he obtained a patent.

In 1785 Daniel Jucaud came from Cognac and established a faiencerie at St. Cybard, a suburb of Angoulême. He was associated with Pierre Fleurat. In

1808, Daniel's son, Jacques Jucaud married Rose Fleurat. At Jacques' death in 1849, his son succeeded him until the factory closed in 1869.

Callaud - Belisle

The Callaud-Belisle factory was in production from 1782 - 1820.

Garrive & Mouchard

In 1790, Jean Garrive was a worker at the Sazerac or the Jucaud factory. In 1792, he established a secondary faiencerie and managed both of them. In 1806, Jean and Henri Garrive directed the production together. In 1808, Louis Mouchard came to the firm. The faiencerie closed in 1822.

Vaumort & Nicollet

In 1815, Jean Vaumort and his son worked at the faiencerie of Jean-Baptiste Glaumont-Sazerac. Then from 1840 to 1850 Vaumort was associated with François Nicollet. In 1853, Nicollet and his son were registered as potters. In 1863, Jean Marphil is added to the register. Angel Taffet succeeded Marphil in 1891.

The production of Angoulême relied heavily on imitations of Moustiers. The houses of Garrive, Mouchard, also Jacques Jucaud produced yellow grotesque and hunchbacked Chinese *(chinois bossu)* patterns.

The production of the Sazerac house is best known for its lions in polychrome, standing with a paw on a fleur-de-lys shield. Sazerac also produced other animals for garden and interior decoration. The firm made pharmacy jars, gourds, bowls, little shoes, salad and soup dishes, and religious objects. The quality of the clay was usually fine, sometimes granular, ranging in color from yellowish-gray to grayish-red.

Alfred Renoleau (1854 - 1930)

In 1891, Renoleau founded a faiencerie at Angoulême with a partner, F. Goras. They set up the business in Port de L'Houmeau. In 1895, following a dispute between the principles, the stockholders appointed Goras to be the director of the firm, which he managed until the factory closed in 1898. In the meantime, Renoleau left and set up a new studio on the Route de Bordeaux. In 1896 he took Gustave Genet as associate.

Renoleau's early works were heavily influenced by Palissy's earth tones, animal and reptile forms. The products from this period were signed R. Falder, an anagram of Renoleau's first name and last initial.

Later, Renoleau's faience production became more colorful and more suited to the commercial market. He made plates, cups and saucers, bowls, vases, cachepots, inkwells, jardinières, statuettes and bas-reliefs in both mono and polychrome.

Other artists whom he employed, beside Gustave Genet were: Olivier Bouquinet, Marthe Vergnaud, Lavaud, and the Renard brothers.

In 1906 -1907 Genet left the Renoleau factory to work in Paris with Robert Clain in a small studio in the Rue de la Goutte d'Or. He returned to Angoulême in 1908 and continued painting very fine flowers and ribbon-like designs in delicate pinks and greens on the Renoleau products up to the 1950s.

Alfred Renoleau had married Marie Claire Bourdongle, but they had no children. Renoleau adopted Joseph Roullet, the husband of Marie Bourdongle, Mme. Renoleau's niece. At Renoleau's death in 1930, his adopted son took over the firm. Roullet died in 1956. The factory closed in 1957.

The mark of the Renoleau factory is: 

86. **Angoulême** Fish plate 10 ½" long. Breton figure with horn designed to imitate Quimper product. Marked: St. Malo; Renoleau factory. Early 20th cent. (Private Collection)

Stanislas I (Leszczynski) 1677-1766.

Twice elected King of Poland, he twice resigned the Polish crown. Finally in 1736, after many battles and challenges to his claim, Stanislas abdicated the unstable throne and received the dukedom of Lorraine and Bar as compensation from his son-in-law, Louis XV of France. He settled at Lunéville, where he established the *Academia Stanislai.* The last thirty years of his life were devoted to the study of science and philanthropy. He died in 1766 at the age of 89.

Faiencceries Of The East — Petit Feu Tradition

The faiences of the East: Strasbourg, Lunéville, and St. Clément, arose out of different traditions from those which influenced the other great faience centers of France. The products of Nevers, inspired by Italians and created by Italian potters retained an Italian flavor. The styles of Rouen, adapted from the Orient and made uniquely French by the support of the King and the nobles, do not figure in the development of the eastern potters. Instead, these eastern faience makers looked to their Dutch, Flemish and German neighbors for inspiration and popular markets. There were geographical, political and economic reasons for this.

Since the invasion of the Teutonic tribes in the 3rd and 4th centuries A.D., Alsace and Lorraine had been Germanic territories. Their proximity to the Swiss, the Dutch, the Belgians, coupled with their use of the natural waterways of the Rhine and the Moselle, kept the focus of their trade and tradition facing eastward rather than toward France.

Though the city of Strasbourg in Alsace had been secured to France in 1648, neither Alsace nor Lorraine would consider themselves part of the French kingdom, nor particularly pro-French until the end of the 18th century, when the revolutionary spirit and the patriotic fervor that Napoleon inspired brought the people of Alsace and Lorraine into the French nation. From 1789 to 1871 the ties between Alsace-Lorraine and France became stronger and more integrated.

In the first quarter of the 18th century, Léopold, duc de Lorraine built his duchy into a flourishing community. By wise economic moves he encouraged his population to grow, and he developed the manufactures of material stuffs, lace, glass and paper. This period of growth coincides with the development of the faiencerie at Lunéville under Chambrette.

In 1735, at Léopold's death, his son, Francis was engaged to marry one of the Hapsburg duchesses. Louis XV of France was not eager to see this neighboring duchy become part of the Austrian Empire, so he cleverly arranged with Francis to exchange the duchy of Tuscany for the duchy of Lorraine. Louis XV then placed his father-in-law, Stanislas Lesczynski, the dethroned King of Poland, as ruler of Lorraine. Ensconced in the charming palace at Lunéville, Stanislas conducted a brilliant little court, founded libraries and ruled benevolently; but Louis XV controlled the financial administration of the estates. At Stanislas' death in 1766, the duchy of Lorraine was joined to France.

At the disasterous end of the Franco-Prussian War (1870 - 1871), the Germans took possession of Alsace-Lorraine as a prize of war. Despite their Germanic roots, these captives resented and resisted German control. On September 30, 1872, the day when the people of Alsace-Lorraine had to decide either to become German citizens or to move away from their homes, 45,000 left their homes to move to France. This territory was not returned to France until after the First World War.

Lunéville - St. Clément

After the Hannong family died out in Strasbourg, (see page 22) around the turn of the 19th century, there were no further important faience developments in Alsace. This fact led to the growth of interest in the faienceries in Lorraine at St. Clément and Lunéville.

The faiencerie at Lunéville was founded in 1723 by Jacques Chambrette, son of a faiencier in Dijon. Many small *ateliers* had been in production in the area since 1718; Chambrette brought them together under the protection of Léopold, duc de Lorraine.

In 1748, Chambrette discovered the process of making demi-porcelain from *terre de pipe,* the very white *"terre de Lorraine".* King Stanislas granted him letters of patent in 1749 which authorized him to start a factory producing this ware. The two factories were joined and designated *"Manufacture Royale".*

In 1757, Chambrette bought property in St. Clément, about eight miles away in the territory of the Three Bishoprics. From here Chambrette was able to export his wares at about one seventh the cost of exporting his Lunéville products. (The export duty on wares leaving Lunéville was 20 livres on a quintal, or 100 kilograms of weight. The duty on goods leaving St. Clément was 3 livres on a quintal.)

Chambrette died in 1757, shortly after the factories merged. His wife and son, Gabriel, and son-in-law, Charles Loyal, took over the establishment. Unfortunately, M. Loyal was less of a business man than an artist; several family disagreements arose and the

87. **Lunéville-St. Clément** Plate 9½" diameter. Revolutionary theme: *"Le peuple commence à murmurer contre les terroristes 1794".* Late 19th cent. (Private Collection)

88. **Lunéville-St. Clément** Plate 9½" diameter. Revolutionary these: *"Pillage des caves royales (1793)".* Late 19th cent. (Private Collection)

business went to court for settlement. In 1763, the St. Clément faiencerie was bought up by Charles Loyal, Richard Mique, King Stanislas' leading architect, and Paul-Louis Cyfflé, the royal sculptor. Cyfflé sold out his shares within the year, but continued to work for Lunéville. He produced a series of well-known statues, *"Cries de Paris", "L'Oiseau Mort", "La Cruche Cassée"*, inspired by Greuze, plus many others which were copied copiously throughout the 19th century.

89. Lunéville-St. Clément Plate 8" diameter. Peasant figure with sponged tree decoration. Border is in characteristic, blue, diamond-shaped design. Early 20th cent. (Private Collection)

In 1772 Loyal disappeared from both factories. Richard Mique formed an association with three others: François Hurtevin de Montauban, Finiels de Saint Albert, and Claude-Charles Rainssant. The factory continued under these men and their descendants, though the production declined greatly. First, the disastrous Treaty of 1786 with England heavily favored the English ware to the detriment of the French products. Secondly, the Revolution interfered with marketing the ware. Thirdly, the factory personnel were drafted away to fight in Napoleon's *Armée du Rhin.* In spite of these setbacks, St. Clément artists produced some new designs based on Revolutionary themes; the most important being the Tree of Liberty and the old cock perched on the fence proclaiming vigilance.

90. Lunéville-St. Clément Demitasse and saucer. Marked: France. Early 20th cent. (Private Collection)

At the beginning of the 19th century, a M. Rousseau revived production at the factory. In 1824, Germain Thomas took over the direction of the St. Clément establishment. From 1826 to 1835, M. Aubry, a modeler at St. Clément, managed the business which at that point entered into a period of prosperity.

In 1840 three of the Thomas sons inherited the business which continued in the family until nearly the end of the century. At that time the Keller family, who had owned and directed the Lunéville factory since the end of the 18th century, bought out the St. Clément business. Again the factories were joined; this time under the mark: Keller and Guérin.

While the Lunéville factory started thirty-four years before the one at St. Clément, both developed along similar lines. The early production of St. Clément was not marked (for tariff reasons?) and so today is indistinguishable from the Lunéville production. Both faienceries supplied the local markets and fairs; both specialized in folk pottery, decorated with the flower baskets and proud coqs of the region. These designs so reflected the sentiments of Lorraine and Alsace that during the period of German occupation (1871 - 1919) those who had remained in Alsace-Lorraine guarded their faience as a special heritage and a patriotic souvenir until the day of their reunion with France.

In 1922, the Fenal family, directors of the faiencerie at Badonviller, took over most of the Keller and Guérin holdings. These three factories were joined that year, but they did not use the three names together — Lunéville-St. Clément-Badonviller until 1962.

As of October 1984, the company *Faïenceries de Lunéville-Badonviller-St. Clément"* maintains its headquarters in Lunéville, but the factory there was closed in 1978. The factory in St. Clément makes the traditional

91. **Lunéville** Plate 9½" diameter. Marked: K et G Lunéville France. Early 20th cent. (Private Collection)

92. **Lunéville** Plate 9½" diameter. Marked: K et G Lunéville France. Early 20th cent. (Private Collection)

French ware, while the other factories in the organization make the following products:

Badonviller	ordinary plates
Digoin	hotel ware
Salins	contemporary tableware
Sarreguemines	tiles
Vitry-le-François	sanitary ware (bathroom fixures)

Sarreguemines

Another faience center which belongs to the Alsace-Lorraine tradition is the factory at Sarreguemines. Founded in 1778 at the junction of the Sarre and the Blise rivers by the Jacobi brothers and Joseph Fabry, the original factory employed fifteen workers for two kilns. Things were to change abruptly when Jacobi hired François-Paul Utzschneider in 1794 to head his faience production.

Utzschneider was born in 1771 in Rieden, Upper Bavaria. At a young age, he went to Sarreguemines to stay with his uncle, who then sent him to England to study ceramics. He returned to Sarreguemines in the midst of the French Revolution. With great energy and vision Utzschneider caused the modest factory to grow and expand to 100 workers in 1800. His technical skill and marketing ability led to many gold medals for the Sarreguemines factory.

In 1836 Utzschneider retired and brought in his son-in-law, the baron Alexandre de Geiger, as his successor. Geiger ran the factory until 1871 when the Franco-Prussian War put Sarreguemines into German territory. To keep the French workmen and to avoid heavy export taxes, two subsidiary factories were created: one at Digoin in 1876; the other at Vitry-le-François in 1881. From the 1880s on Sarreguemines products were marked: with D for Digoin and V for Vitry.

In 1871, Geiger's son, Paul, took direction of the Sarreguemines factory until 1913. After the First World War, the three factories were united. Vitry became a manufacturing center for stove tiles and bathroom furnishings.

During the Second World War, all the buildings at Sarreguemines were destroyed and reconstructed in a new area on the right bank of the Sarre.

It is not clear whether the faienciers at Sarreguemines ever used a true faience *pâte* at the beginning of their production, but it is sure that Utzschneider brought back from England the knowledge of manufacturing *faïence fine.* Most of the ware that is not of special composition: "Wedgwood", jasperware, *grès,* etc. was made of *faïence fine,* composed of the fine white clay from across the Rhine. The decorations were done in several ways: by hand, *au pinceau* — with special brushes by experienced painters, *au pochoir,* with a sponge or a daub, *au tampon,* with a template and *à l'impression,* by printing in one form or another.

The technique of printing on glazed china came from England. Around 1806, Lambert, a faiencier from Sèvres, succeeded in reproducing an engraving on faience. He won a prize for his efforts. At first all the impressions on faience were made in monochrome — black or *bistre* (tawny colored). By 1809, experiments by Neppel were made in color reproductions, but these would not work reliably for another twenty-five years.

The impression method required an artist's original be engraved on a copper plate — either directly on the bare copper, or on a thin layer of varnish covering the copper. From the copper plate the design would be transferred to a special paper which was placed on the ceramic object. The back of the paper was sponged with water so that the image adhered to the object (usually a plate). The plate was then fired at over 500° which fixed the impression. The decoration was varnished and then fired a second time.

Sarreguemines also used the stone lithograph procedure, whereby the original was carved into stone tiles for printing. This method was used long after the Second World War. At present, seriographs are made on silk or nylon screens.

Throughout the 200 years of its existence, Sarreguemines has neglected no area of ceramic production. Its products included plates with floral designs, roosters, fruits, country scenes; prints of scenes from daily life, comical, historical, literary, folklore or religious themes. It has been said that by the end of the 19th century no French household was without some piece of Sarreguemines. The success of the factory lay in the variety, high quality and low cost of its wares.

93. Sarreguemines Advertising tile 11¾ x 6¼". Marked: Sarreguemines D V. Early 20th cent. (Private Collection)

Though the type of ware made at these eastern factories was not the special, extravagant product such as was made for the royal and the rich at the old, revered centers, this pottery was a folk product, designed for the common people. Lunéville and St. Clément specialized in ordinary tableware decorated with flower baskets (the earliest design was called "Maikrug"), flowers, animals, geometrics and most importantly, the "coq fier", the proud cock which represents vigilance and virility.

These wares were transported throughout the countryside by *colporteurs* who carried them in large straw baskets, *hottes,* on their backs, or by wagons to the local fairs and weekly markets. Considered very popular, but not great, these faiences appealed to the plain people of modest means. The plates served as prizes in the shooting contests at the fairs; they were bought as wedding presents suitable for a newly-wed couple to hang in their kitchen. These faiences appeared regularly at the *"messti"* or local festivals — a prize plate from such a festival was known as a *"Messtideller"* and would be considered of great sentimental value.

Throughout the 19th century, as the production of this faience became more economical, series of plates, pitchers, soup tureens, and complete services would be available. In 1820, stamps, imprints and decals began to be used in addition to or to replace hand painting. In 1835-1840, painted scenes became prevalent: copies of religious art, scenes of popular history, military and Napoleonic themes. Around 1860, the plates took on sayings, such as *"Sei Glucklish",* or *"Sois Heureux", "Aus Liebe"* or *"Par Amour".* Pitchers might say *"Sei niemals leer"* — never be empty! These scenes and sayings could be swiftly and economically applied with decals or stencils.

Living on the frontier, this faience reflects many German aspects: the use of the local dialect and/or German; the use of fine clays which make this ware resemble Meissen more often than other French faiences; the use of the *petit feu* method to produce pinks and clear greens, which again differs from the *grand feu* French faiences; the early production of small statues and table ornaments, a tradition more German than French. Thus, the faience of Lorraine presents an interesting blend of German technology with a French flavor — a creation which speaks with a very local accent.

Conclusion

The art of French faience making in the 19th and 20th centuries was subject to profound technical, cultural and social changes which arose out of the industrial revolution. We have seen how the invention of machines affected all phases of faience work from the excavation of clays to the blending and preparation of the glazes for the finished product. Steam replaced foot power to drive the potters' wheels; new methods of kiln loading ensured a greater success rate in the firing, and the introduction of gas as fuel in 1847, enabled potters to produce more items at less cost.

At the same time, industrialization was creating a new society of entrepreneurs, bankers, financiers and merchants. Gaxotte, the historian, has defined this group as "an opinionated, energetic class of people, aware of their merits and convinced of their rights." From 1830, this process of democratization, begun by the revolution and fostered by industrial progress and the widening of the economy, gave this middle class access to areas of art and luxury which had heretofore been reserved for kings and nobles. Royal residences and possessions were put on display to the public: the museum at Sèvres, in 1829; the palace of Versailles, in 1837.

Improvements in the printing process allowed for publication of pictures, reproductions of paintings and original fine art which fostered the production of magazines and revues. *Magasin pittoresque,* in 1833; *Illustration,* in 1843.

The problem of mass production for a much larger popular market was often solved by simplification of the product design. In other words, where the 18th century factory had produced a single, elegant and perfect item on royal command, the 19th and 20th century factories had to produce many items at lower cost to satisfy a consumer of modest means. This was achieved, particularly by those factories which continued to hand paint, by reducing the size of the piece, e.g. making a miniature (vase, statue, musical instrument, or animal form) or by lessening the amount of detail on a larger piece.

Hand in hand with mass production for an increased population came a new concern for the distribution of goods. The opening of new resorts after the 1830s (Trouville, Deauville, Etretat, Dieppe, etc.), the development of rail lines to beaches, spas, casinos and other attractions for a vacationing public, provided new outlets for the faience producers. *Bibelots* and miniatures bearing the resort's name could be sold as souvenirs. Candy stores and gift shops would carry faience bowls filled with *dragées* (sugared almonds) and fancy *bonbons.*

By the end of the 19th century, two separate themes in art had developed: 1) a nostalgic desire to recreate the glorious items of the past (this was being done at the faienceries mentioned above); 2) a complete departure from the past, emphasizing art forms which reflected the new ideas of the industrial age.

Through magazine pictures and actual museum visits, the public became aware of historical treasures and luxurious things which they now coveted for themselves. If the most precious and costly items were beyond their grasp, the new bourgeoisie could at least attain the appearance of *luxe.* Machines could make replicas of fine furnishings, simulated leather, printed rather than woven fabrics, reproductions of all kinds. All these might be advertised in the local papers. *Figaro,* founded in 1848, was the first to sell advertising space for the promotion of goods. Advertising art and poster production emerged at this time as a new art form to serve industry.

In the years 1850-1870, Haussmann, the urban

architect, transformed Paris into a modern, elegant city. His creation of boulevards and strolling areas led to the development of galleries and the founding of new department stores, *les Grands Magasins: Au Bon Marché* in 1852, *Le Grand Dépot,* in 1860, *La Samaritaine,* in 1871, *Le Printemps,* in 1881. The rue du Paradis-Poissonière became the fashionable street for luxury items in glass, porcelain and pottery.

As the public's desire grew for amusing *bibelots* and fine reproductions of old faience, centers such as Blois, Desvres, Malicorne and Quimper catered to this market by making molds similar to the old designs and by re-creating the famous décors of Rouen, Moustiers and Nevers.

Of the two influences, *passéist* and *art moderne,* the second expressed greater vitality. The modern movement in faience produced many innovative artists who entered their works in the International Expositions, and exhibited in galleries and specialty shops such as *Primavera.* Supported by the patronage of the new bourgeois entrepreneurs, these creative faienciers were able to produce unique objects in special clays, *grès, métallique, barbotines* and *faïence fine* with some hope of selling them. Nevertheless, these artists often protected themselves financially by making the souvenir and *fantaisie* pieces that were the sure sellers. It was not unusual for a potter to produce both *avant-guard* items and souvenir bric-a-brac at the same time, in the same kiln. In the mid 1930s, four out of every five pieces of faience produced at the Gojon factory in Haute Savoie were *fantaisie* items. These were the pieces which paid for the production of the other one.

Renoleau from Angoulême had a merchant distributer in the Charente-Maritime region for his popular pieces; Balon from Blois marketed his trinkets throughout France; Pisareff from Normandy sold many small faience pieces through a Mme. Prével, a *confiseur* in Caen.

The late 19th and early 20th centuries experienced active cross currents in art and industry. The entrepreneur became a collector of fine, unique items. He also became aware of the influence of art in his work; he realized that his product, whatever it may be, must have some aesthetic value of its own. Industrial and commercial artists came into factory production and influenced the design and advertising of the products. Art had entered business.

By the same token, business entered the art field. No longer supported by royal patronage, the artist had to market his creation by seeking the support of the public. According to Albert Boime, there are many points of similarity between the artist and the entrepreneur. Both are in business for themselves, engaged in a risk-taking operation which only pays off if the end-product succeeds in an unpredictable marketplace, affected by numerous changing phenomena.

In many instances, the artist faiencier had to learn the ways of an entrepreneur to stay in business. He had to develop publicity materials, catalogues and advertisements; he had to market his wares in the resort areas, at fairs and local celebrations. He had to produce popular merchandise or products for commercial use in addition to his important items. Examples of these are the ceramic ashtrays advertising liquors, etc. or publicity items for a particular restaurant or manufacturing firm; miniature kitchenware which the faienciers produced after enamel ware replaced the traditional *grès* and stoneware as basic cooking utensils; ceramic containers for mustard, apple brandy, etc. which were made to promote the contents rather than to promote the faiencerie. Faienciers used all of these strategies to continue their operations and occasionally to produce serious art work.

Art experts and curators are understandably disparaging when it comes to discussing the merits of the secondary art work of these faienciers. They consider the *fantaisie* items "potboilers" and of no consequence. On the other hand, these items have a particular historic charm and value. They have contributed substantially to the cultural education of the public; they have allowed for the creation of more "significant" art, which is produced for the few at high cost. Finally, the *fantaisie* pieces have provided us with objects of sentimentality, nostalgia and simple pleasure. That is not an achievement to be scorned.

94. CA Group of Royal Busts. Left: Anne de Bretagne, 5"tall, wife of Louis XII; center: Louis XII, 8" tall; right: Claude de France 5¾" tall, daughter of Anne and Louis, wife of François I.
(Private Collection)

CA

In the course of researching the material for this book, we had hoped to come across the identity and origin of a faience popularly called CA. Unfortunately, we have no definite proofs and correlations to make which would solve the mystery once and for all; instead we have some negative conclusions to offer and a few possibilities.

The faience in question is a *grand feu* product, characterized by a deep red clay, covered with a grayish, crackled glaze and decorated with a strong, dark blue, a thick red and a light yellow coloring. The border designs often include a loop and dot pattern; the secondary decorations include a two-toned yellow and orange fleur-de-lys and a blue and green stylized ermine tail.

In the collection of fifty or so pieces with which we are most familiar, five basic decorative designs appear:
1) Emblems of the Loire Valley which include items bearing the picture of a salamander breathing fire (this is the blazon of François I); the ermine of Anne de Bretagne; the *porc-épic* of Louis XII, and the swan, pierced with an arrow, the blazon of both Claude de France and her mother-in-law, Louise de Savoie. Many of these items are also marked Blois, Amboise, Chambord — all royal châteaux tourist attractions in the Loire Valley. In addition, this faiencerie made busts of all the aforementioned kings and queens.
2) Armorial decorations which appear on series of plates and on individual *fantaisie* items. Sometimes the designs represent actual town coats-of-arms; other times the decorations are purely fictional.
3) Emblems of Canada — particularly Quebec — which include mottos, such as *"Je me Souviens"* and represen-

95. CA Jardinière 9¼" x 5". Red clay and typical coloration of this unknown factory. Royal crest of François I. (Private Collection)

tations of the golden dog. Also this CA factory produced busts of Canadian personalities: Champlain and Laval. 4) Mottos and provincial emblems, such as the blazon of Brittany and ermine tail designs; also the double barred cross and the thistles of Lorraine on souvenir items. 5) Country scenes — one depicting a shepherd on the hillside; another showing a fishing scene.

96. CA Woman figure double salt 8½" tall. Red clay, crackled glaze, strong blue and red loop and dot design with fleur-de-lys and ermine tails. Factory unknown. (Private Collection)

All of these productions are signed with an interlaced CA which is not consistently the hand of one artist. The mark sometimes also includes a number — this suggests a factory of some size which recorded its molds.

Though a number of collectors have thought that these pieces were products of the Quimper factory, we are certain that they are not. Information from retired personnel, a study of the records, and conversations with Michel Roullot, the Quimper expert, all agree that this CA has no relation at all with Quimper.

Looking into various books on marks and signatures, we have to discard any CA marks which relate to 17th and 18th century faience because the items we are researching are late 19th and early 20th century products. We know this because several pieces can be positively dated 1908, the year of the 300th anniversary of the founding of Quebec. Our best guess is that the factory produced from 1880 to 1930, more or less.

Among the CA or AC possibilities listed under marks and signatures we find three artists whom we have researched. The first Auguste Chauvigné (1829-1904) of Tours signed his work: CA We went to Tours to the museum there and looked at Chauvigné's work. Several pieces on display revealed a Palissy-type faience with snakes, lizards, bugs, etc. in grand relief on platters and monuments. This work bore no resemblance to the faience in question. The curators who examined our photos could not enlighten us at all.

Since many of the Loire Valley items are marked Blois, we went on to the museum at Blois and interviewed the curator, Mme. de Mallerais. She took us through the museum's reserve collections; she inspected our photos; we discussed possibilities at length, but she could not identify the faience. She is positive it is not a Blois faiencerie.

The next possibility which was suggested by several sources was the entrepreneur Charles Ahrenfeldt. This man (1807-1894) was an exporter of porcelain from Limoges. He acquired a factory in Altrohlau in Bohemia, and during the 1880s he began to produce his own porcelain from sources in the Limoges area. Primarily an entrepreneur, he built a large exportation business to Germany, London, New York and San Francisco. His son Charles Ahrenfeldt, Jr. (1857-1934) enlarged the capacity of the factories and expanded the lucrative export business to America.

Though the signature  is reminiscent of the mark we are searching, the product of this association is porcelain rather than faience and the patterns of decoration bear no correlation.

Third on our list to investigate was the family Chaumeil. Henri Curtil's book, Marques et Signatures de la Faïence Française shows an Alcide Chaumeil in Paris (1847-1919) who signed his work  also a Henri Chaumeil (1877-1944) whose signature is  A trip to the publisher proved that M. Curtil is dead and can not give us any further information on how and where he discovered Chaumeil's examples or signatures. Since M. Curtil's references on Quimper are flawed, we are inclined to question the validity of the Chaumeil information.

In the *Musée des Arts dècoratifs,* there are several collections of periodicals in at least three different libraries. Concentrating on the periodicals from 1890 to 1930, we looked for articles, gallery reviews, pictures of current exhibits, etc. which would form a positive connection between Chaumeil and the faience we had in hand. Though we found some pictures of Chaumeil's work, none of them resembled the highly decorated faience we were looking for. The examples shown in the periodicals included artistic *grès* ware and several vases, *objets d'art,* in a monochrome white glaze.

In the magazine L'Art Vivant, Nov. 1928, we came across an article by Tisserand on Henri Chaumeil. Though the thrust of the discussion was on the modern art pottery that Chaumeil himself produced, pieces such as those for which we had seen pictures, a glancing mention was made of the "general production of his *ateliers* where the workers make remarkable copies of the old faience".

This is a very thin string of evidence, if it is worth anything at all. We are still not satisfied that a positive connection has been made between CA and the Chaumeil factory.

Taking a different tack, we decided to run down our Canadian leads with the hope of establishing records for a factory or an importer there.

The first, obvious connection had to do with the CA design of a yellow dog, lying down with a bone in its paws. The verse under the picture is as follows:

"Je suis un chien qui ronge lo
En le rongeant je prend mon repos
Un tems viendra qui n'est pas venu
que je mordray qui m'aura mordu."
1736

"I am a dog who chews the bone
While chewing it I take my rest.
A time will come which is not yet come
when I will bite the one who has bitten me."

97. **CA** Golden Dog figure 4½" long. Quebec inscription on pedestal. Factory unknown. Circa 1908. (Private Collection)

The verse is awkward and the tense of the last verb spoils the dictum, but the general meaning conveys a definite threat.

First we discovered that the plaque of this dog and his saying can be seen today over the main door of the Quebec General Post Office. It had been moved there when the original residence was torn down. Next, we discovered that the dog is known as the Golden Dog (Le Chien d'Or), not the yellow dog as we had assumed from the color of the faience.

The legend of the Golden Dog is very popular in Quebec, though there are many variations on the theme. Stories dating from 1769 to 1915 tell of at least six different controversies which might have been associated with the plaque's meaning. Basically, most of the stories involve disputes and threats of revenge between certain town officials and Dr. Roussell, the original owner of the house on which the plaque was found.

In Les Cahiers des Dix, 1945, Pierre-Georges Roy published an article, *"L'Histoire Vrai du Chien D'Or"* whose explanation is currently accepted as the most accurate. According to Roy, a similar statue of a dog, circa 1650, exists in Pézenas, in southern France on the garden gate of a M. Delbousquet's estate. Roussell, who originally came from the area of Pézenas undoubtedly knew this statue and probably duplicated it as a simple remembrance of his native land. The fact that the verses of the Canadian version scan less correctly than those of the Pézenas monument, Roy explains as a case of poor memory. Roy feels that Roussell probably placed the plaque and the verses as best he could recall them on the new addition he made to his house in 1736.

The verse on the CA faience has been taken from the Quebec plaque rather than from the Pézenas version; therefore, we feel it was made for the Canadian market.

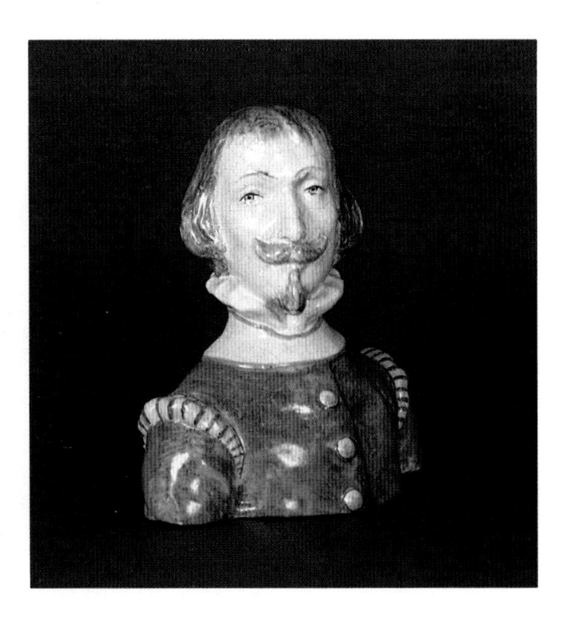

98. **CA** Bust of Champlain 5½" tall. Marked: Champlain 1567-1635 1608 - 1908. The first pair of dates refer to Champlain's birth and death. 1608 is the date of the founding of Quebec; 1908 is the tercentenary. Factory unknown. (Private Collection)

In 1908 Quebec celebrated the 300th anniversary of its founding by Champlain and the 200th anniversary of the death of Laval, the first Bishop of New France. According to the minutes in the Archives, preparation for the celebration began late and with some hesitation. As late as January 1908, there was still a possibility that the festivities would be held in 1909. In favor of 1908 there were those who wished to combine the celebration of the anniversaries with the erection of a statue of Laval. Others favored an August celebration when the weather would be agreeable and the harvest would show to best advantage. The king of England was invited, but His Majesty could not attend. The Prince of Wales agreed to represent the Mother Country, but he could only be present for the last ten days of July. The celebration dates were thus fixed for July 21st to July 31st. The minutes of the planning meetings detail arrangements for commemorative postage stamps and official souvenir booklets, postcards and buttons. These are later advertised in the Quebec newspapers. Though we have in hand two CA busts, one of Champlain and the other of Laval, each with their dates and also the date 1908, we have not been able to find any orders in the minutes for this type of commemorative faience.

As we have indicated above, plans for the celebration were rather tentative. Genuinely afraid that too much advanced publicity would draw too many visitors for available housing, the planners deliberately underpublicized the event at the outset. Though the daily papers are complete for the year, the minutes of the planning group end abruptly on April 24th. We find no other references to commemorative faience items and no advertisements for them in the daily papers. We can draw no firm conclusions on the basis of what is available in the archives at Quebec.

The coat of arms of Quebec and the motto, *"Je me Souviens"* appear on several CA pieces we have seen. The design of the Quebec shield was assigned by Queen Victoria in 1868; however the motto was not added to the official emblem until 1883. Therefore the production of these CA pieces must be after 1883. This is in keeping with our estimate that the CA factory was in operation around 1880 - 1930, more or less.

When we were in Blois, we noticed in a gift shop several items whose decoration resembled the CA loop and dot design. The décor was similar, but the clay was gray rather than red. The owner of the shop told us these were items ordered from Desvres. On our trip to Desvres, a representative of Masse Frères recognized the singing frog figure as one Masse had produced at one time. Their version had differed slightly in that it had no side baskets in the mold.

99. CA Figure of singing frog 4¾" tall. Deep red clay, crackled glaze, typical CA coloration. Side basket marked Blois also bears ermine emblem of Anne de Bretagne. Piece is marked CA 746. (Private Collection)

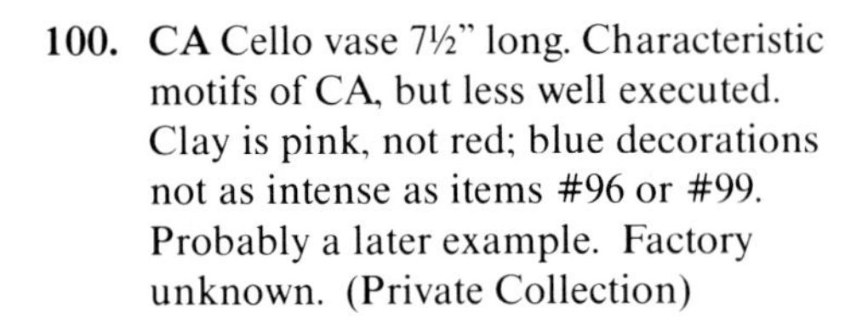

100. CA Cello vase 7½" long. Characteristic motifs of CA, but less well executed. Clay is pink, not red; blue decorations not as intense as items #96 or #99. Probably a later example. Factory unknown. (Private Collection)

We have also seen other pieces with CA's characteristic pattern marked Géo Martel. The conclusion we have drawn is that the original, red clay CA went out of business in the 1930s, but similiar items continued to be produced in imitation by the expert copyists at Desvres. This would account for the difference in the clay, the lack of crackle and the less forceful execution of the designs we see on what we believe to be more recent pieces.

In conclusion, we feel that no positive connection has been made between the very distinctive, red clay, crackled glaze CA faience and a specific factory. Many people have offered suggestions or opinions, but these have withered in the strong light of on-site investigation. The search goes on!

Angoulême

Lassuze
1882

Pineau and Patros
1888

Renoleau
(1900-1930)

Blois

(1861-1889)

(1890-1929)

Ulysse à Blois
9 Bruneau Balon
Sre d'E. Balon

G. Bruneau-Balon-Blois

(1930)

(1873-1881)

Adrien Thibault (1875-1918)

Boulogne

Verlingue
(1903-1920)

L↓V

Louis & Verlingue
(1910)

H↓D

Henri Delcourt
(1920 -)

Creil Montereau

1880

Desvres

Formaintraux-Courquin
(1872-1934)

Fourmaintraux frères
(1877-1887)

Gabriel Fourmaintraux
(1900-1934)

FAIENCERIE D'ART
Décor Main

MASSE FRÈRES
DESVRES

Géo Martel
(1900-)

Gien

(1856-1860)

(1860-1871)

Gien, cont.

1871-1875

1875-1935

1938-1960

1941-1960

GIEN
FRANCE

1960-1971

GIEN
FRANCE

since 1971

Lunéville St. Clément

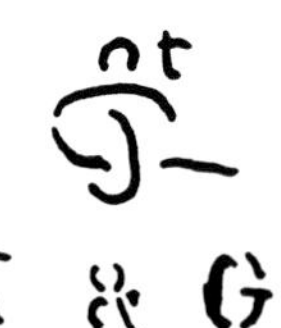

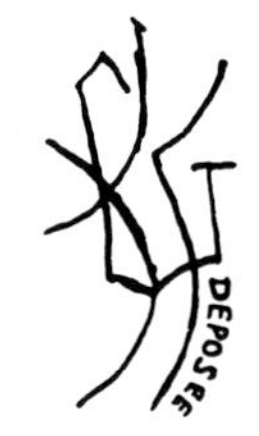

Currently in use with date

Malicorne

PBx

Pouplard/Béatrix (1895-1952)

Tessier (1924-in current use)

Marseilles

Veuve Perrin (1748-1795)

Twentieth century reproductions continue to use this mark.

Moustiers in current production

De Peyre
Feret
J.M.V. Fine
Garnier

Morée-Méret
St. Michel
de Ségriès
Stefani á St. Jurs

Martes-Tolosane

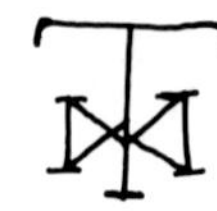

Reproductions of Moustiers designs

Nevers

Antoine Montagnon (1875-1889)

Antoine Montagnon (1889-1899)

Gabriel Montagnon (1899-1937)

F.E. Cottard 1922

Jean Montagnon (1937-1978)

Quimper			
Porquier	P Porquier (1860-1870)	PB Porquier (Beau) (1875-1905)	AP Adolph Porquier (1875-1905)

de la Hubaudière Grande Maison HB				
	HB Hubaudière (1860-1870)	HB (1883-1904)	HB impressed (1898-1904)	HB Quimper (1904-1984)
HB (1920-1950)	HB ODETTA (1922)	Quimper (1939)	HB (1954)	HB Quimper France entièrement décoré main (1968-1984)

Henriot			
	HR (1894-1904)	HR Quimper (1904-1922)	HenRiot QUIMPER (1922-1984)
PB Quimper (1915-1930s)	HENRIOT QUIMPER FRANCE entièrement décoré main (1968-1984)	HB HenRiot Quimper France Peint main (1984-)	

Marks used on items commissioned for a particular shop

Made by HB for Macy's New York in the 1930s

Made for Kenilworth Studios (?) by HenRiot in the 1930s

N. S. & . S
HB
QUIMPER
FRANCE

Made for N.S & .S (?) by HB in the 1930s

FIRESIDE
HenRiot
Quimper
FRANCE

Usually on yellow items

Quimper, cont.

Fouillen

P. Fouillen
Quimper
G

Keraluc

Keraluc
prés Quimper

Rouen

See Tardy for a long list of 18th century marks.

ROUEN

(in blue, often accompanied by a number in black)
Late 19th or 20th century reproduction; probable Desvres.

Items with a Rouen town crest also often bear the mark Rouen, but this has no relation to the location of the manufacture.

Sarreguemines

1800-1850

19th century

1876

D representing the addition of Dignon
V representing the addition of Vitry
1880

Strasbourg

See Tardy for 18th century marks.

Reproductions made currently by Lunéville St. Clèment.

Bibliography

Albis, Jean and Romanet, Celeste. La Porcelaine de Limoges. Sous le Vent, 1980.

Artel, Martine. "St. Clément et sa Faïencerie." in Revue Lorraine Populaire. fév. 1981.

Barbier, Jean. "Faïence Fine de Creil et Montereau." in Estampille. #185 oct. 1985.

Boime, Albert. "Entreprenurial Patronage." in Enterprise and Entrepreneurs in 19th and 20th century France. eds Carter, Forster and Moody. John Hopkins University Press, 1976.

Bondhus, Sandra. Quimper Pottery: A French Folk Art Faïence. 1981.

Chaffers, William. Marks and Monograms on Pottery and Porcelain. Los Angeles: Borden Publishing Company.

Cox, Warren. The Book of Pottery and Porcelain. Revised Edition. New York: Crown Publishers, Inc., 1975.

Curtil, Henri. Marques et Signatures de la Faïence Française. Paris: Charles Massin, 1969.

Dauguet, Claire and Guilleme-Brulon, Dorothée. Reconnaître les Origines des Faïences. Paris: Charles Massin.

de Plas, Solange. Les Faïences de Rouen, du Nord et de la Région Parisienne. Paris: Charles Massin.
Les Faïences de Nevers et du Centre de la France. Paris: Charles Massin.

Després, P. L'Art du Potier - La Faïence. Serg, 1976.

Durand, Philippe. "Les Poteries de Malicorne." in Estampille. #171-172 juillet-août, 1984.

Ernould-Gandouet. M. La Céramique en France au 19e Siècle. Paris: Grund, 1969.

Fleming, John and Honour, Hugh. Dictionary of the Decorative Arts. New York: Harper and Row, 1977.

Giacomotti, Jeanne. Faïences Françaises. Le Livre Partout, 1963.

Gillard, M.C. "La Faïence de Gien." in Estampille. #184 sept. 1985.

Jacob, Alain. Les Faïences du Nord. #1 ABC Collections. Numéro hors-série, avril, 1979.

Klein, Georges. "Quand les Faïenciers de Lorraine séduisent l'Alsace." in ABC Décor. #233-234 juillet-août, 1984.

Labour, Joseph. La Céramique Bretonne. Conde-sur-Noireau: Corlet, 1980.

Lajoix, Anne. La Céramique en France (1925-1947). Paris: Sous le Vent, 1983.

Lane, Arthur. French Faïence. New York: Praeger Publishers, 1970.

Latier, Marcel. Faïences et Faïenciers d'Angoulême. Bordeaux: Imprimeries Delmas, 1971.

Mala, Alain. "La Terre, la Main, le Feu." in Cénomane, Nouvelle Revue Sarthoise. #10 été, 1983.

Pelichet, Edgar and Duperrex, Michele. La Céramique Art Nouveau.
Paris: La Bibliothèque des Arts, éditions du Grand-pont.

Roullot, Michel J. Les Faïences Artistiques de Quimper. Lorient: Art Média, 1980.

Taburet, Marjatta. La Faïence de Quimper. Paris: Sous le Vent, 1979.

Taburet, Marjatta. La Faïence de Nevers. Paris: Sous le Vent, 1981.

Tardy and Lesur, Adrien. Les Poteries et les Faïences Françaises. 3e édition, Paris: Tardy
Angoulême in ABC Décor. #237 nov. 1984.
Malicorne in ABC Décor. #250 Noël 1985.

Tisserand, Ernest. "Henri Chaumeil." in l'Art Vivant. nov. 1928.

Varenne, Gaston. "Colette Gueden ou l'aimable fantaisie." in Art et Décoration. jan. 1933.

Exposition catalogues: La Céramique dans la Région Centre. oct. 1980.
Cent Ans de Faïence à Blois. dec. 1978.

Factory catalogues: Faïenceries de Lunéville-Badonviller-St. Clément. (undated)
Faïenceries de HenRiot. (undated)

Picture Credits

ABC Décor: #85,

Angell Photography: Cover, # 8, 15, 19, 20, 22, 23, 25, 26, 28, 29, 30, 31, 32, 33, 34, 36, 37, 38, 39, 40, 41, 42, 43, 44, 45, 46, 48, 49, 50, 51, 52, 53, 54, 55, 56, 57, 58, 59, 60, 61, 62, 63, 64, 65, 66, 67, 68, 69, 70, 71, 72, 74, 75, 80, 81, 82, 83, 86, 87, 88, 89, 90, 91, 92, 93, 94, 95, 96, 97, 98, 99, 100.

Charles Massin: Les Faïences de Nevers, # 2, 3, 4, 5.
Les Faïences de Rouen, # 10, 11, 12, 13.

Photo Ellebé: # 6.

Index